YOUR HEALING
IS WITHIN
YOU

*A pastoral and scriptural
presentation of
the Healing Ministry of the Church*

YOUR HEALING
IS WITHIN
YOU

by

JIM GLENNON

Distributed by Logos International

U.S. Edition 1980
Printed in the United States of America
Library of Congress Catalog Number: 80-82616
International Standard Book Number: 0-88270-457-5
Distributed by Logos International, Plainfield, NJ 07060

For the members of
St Andrew's Cathedral
Healing Ministry Congregation
with gratitude and affection

and with thanks to
Mac and Esma Job
who re-wrote the pastoral addresses
and made them interesting

"The kingdom of God
is within you"

— *Jesus Christ*

Contents

Foreword

This is a masterly book written by a masterly man.

When I first knew Canon Glennon at St Andrew's Cathedral, Sydney, he was carrying heavy burdens. Every evening, after my lecture was over and the congregation had departed, he and I would pray together, first for the healing of old hurtful memories and then for the fullness of the Spirit. Thus the faith and power in Christ that had always been his were greatly increased, and naturally his healing work at the Cathedral also greatly increased.

Canon Glennon is rooted and grounded in the church. As he is without family responsibilities, the church, and particularly the Cathedral Church of St Andrew, has been the centre of his life. Both in private ministrations and in the weekly Wednesday evening healing services, he has become known world-wide as a quiet, powerful leader in the healing ministry of the Christian church.

I feel privileged in commending his book, and Canon Jim Glennon himself, to the Lord's people everywhere.

Monrovia,   AGNES SANFORD
California

Author's Preface

In October 1972, at the invitation of the Reverend Brian Thewlis of St Paul's Anglican Church in the Melbourne suburb of Malvern, Victoria, I conducted a week-long teaching mission on the ministry of healing. To the praise of God it was a wonderful time. There is something infectious about an enthusiastic crowd come together for a common purpose under the Spirit of God. Certainly his presence and inspiration that week gave great blessing both to speaker and congregation alike.

After the mission, various church and house meetings interested in the healing ministry continued to use the tapes of the mission addresses, but not much more than that might have happened if it had been left to me. Then, some eighteen months later, Christian writers Macarthur and Esma Job, who had attended the mission, finally decided to do something about a conviction they had felt for some time. They believed that the mission addresses had made such an impact, both during the mission itself, and afterwards through the medium of the tape recorder, that they should be published. So they broached the matter to Brian Thewlis, who felt the same guidance and offered to transcribe the recorded addresses as a first step.

Living 500 miles away in Sydney, I knew nothing of this. Yet for the first time in my ministry I had quite independently come to the conclusion that I should publish some of my material. But as I am a speaker rather than a writer, I was hesitant about making a beginning and unsure as to how I should go about it. Mac and Esma's subsequent offer to take on the task of committing the mission addresses to paper and to do any necessary re-writing could hardly have come at a better time, and I accepted at once. So began a happy and creative relationship and I would here express my deep appreciation of all they have done to make the publication of Part 1 of this book possible.

I am also most grateful to others who have made theological, medical and editorial contributions to the preparation of the manuscript as a whole; as well as to those good friends who have so patiently typed and re-typed its pages. As there have been many who have willingly helped in various ways, I hope they will all understand if I express my gratitude to them collectively.

As readers will note, the book is divided into two parts. Part I is devoted to various pastoral aspects of the healing ministry and is liberally illustrated by real-life case histories. Part II is a scriptural exposition of the healing ministry. As far as I know, this is the first time that both a pastoral and scriptural presentation of this ministry has been offered in the one book. Perhaps a word of explanation about the origins of Part II may also be in order.

In 1971, the Diocese of Sydney, to which I have the honour to belong, appointed through its Synod a committee to enquire into the neo-pentecostal movement and the healing ministry. I was a member of the committee and submitted the paper, which basically forms the Part II of this book, setting out the scriptural basis for the church's ministry of healing. The committee later published a report entitled *Both Sides to the Question*, which contained an abridged version of my paper. With the goodwill of the publishers of that report, the full length paper, together with some additional material, is now published for the first time.

I have been on the staff of St. Andrew's Cathedral, Sydney, for 25 years and for 20 of those years the Dean and Chapter have allowed me to develop this ministry in the Cathedral. Their generosity and kindness have been all the more valued because, very likely, it is a ministry which they themselves would not have initiated. Perhaps in this regard I should say that I alone am responsible for the content of the book.

But it is the Healing Ministry Congregation that meets in the Cathedral each Wednesday night at 6 o'clock, who have been my special collaborators in the real work of preparing this book. For what is written has come out of what we have done together. We have been a team, a family, a community — one in which each person has played his or her part in ministry. Words cannot adequately convey what I mean here; but as long as they understand, as I know they do, I am content. Most appropriately the book is dedicated to them.

A.J.G.

Part I

Pastoral Guidelines

1

Does God Still Heal Today?

He has granted to us his precious and very great promises. 2 Peter 1:4

Is any among you sick? Let him call for the elders of the church, and let them pray over him, anointing him with oil in the name of the Lord; and the prayer of faith will save the sick man, and the Lord will raise him up; and if he has committed sins, he will be forgiven.

James 5: 14,15

IS THE HEALING power of God still at work in our world today? Can we be sure that God wants to heal us? Does the sick person need to have faith? What about Paul's thorn in the flesh? These and other questions are most important in any consideration of divine healing. We need to examine them and seek answers — answers that are scriptural and answers that are practical in everyday situations.

But before we set about doing that, let us first look at some real-life examples of healing today in response to believing prayer. To preserve the privacy of the persons mentioned in this book their names and some details have been changed. All the events referred to are known to me personally.

Mark and Dorothy Bailey live in South Australia. With three daughters and their adopted son, Graeme, they were a very happy and united young family. Graeme himself was a jolly little fellow, and as the youngest and the only boy, was very dear to them all.

When Graeme was small he seemed to be a little round-shouldered, but as he grew it became apparent that he had a more serious problem. The local medical practitioner prescribed back exercises; but in spite of this the condition slowly became worse, and a pronounced hump appeared in the upper part of his back. Eventually the advice of a specialist was sought, and the parents were told that the deformity was due to the collapse of several adjacent verte-brae. This was compressing his chest, and his heart was consequently being affected. Little could be done for the lad, as he was already a "hunchback". His future seemed hope-less.

The boy's parents were intelligent Christians, and they realised that if their boy was to be helped in any way, that assistance would have to come from beyond any human resource. This led them to read the Bible with a new interest, and they found that it promised that the prayer of faith would raise up the one who was sick. They realised that if they, as parents, were prepared to keep their promises to their own children, how much more would God, their heavenly father, keep his promises to his earthly children. They became convinced that there was a promise of God for them to claim for their boy, and like the man who brought his son to Jesus, they were not prepared to take "no" for an answer.

Mark and Dorothy looked at Graeme, now almost a teenager, and saw him bent over, distressed and distressing. They had never exercised faith for a mountain that was as big as this — it could scarcely have been bigger — and by comparison their faith seemed so small! But they believed what they had read, and they said to themselves: "God has promised and we are calling on him. We are praying the prayer of faith, and if healing does not come straight away, it will come gradually." They brought these convictions together in an informed and whole-hearted way, so that they truly believed that God was willing and able to heal their son.

At first nothing seemed to happen. Yet they were not discouraged — they just went on believing. After some time they thought that there could be some marginal improvement, and after more time they were sure that there was a small change for the better: "first the blade..."[1] As small change was added to small change, the improvement became more obvious. And so they continued for three whole years, believing for healing and returning thanks to God for the on-going improvement.

It is wonderful to be able to say that by the end of that time their boy had grown completely straight! His chest and heart were normal, and the hump was gone! He subsequently finished his education and trained as a motor mechanic. He has since married, and he and his wife have their own children. And anybody meeting him today would never know that he had once been grossly deformed.

Marion Summers was a member of the Healing Ministry Congregation at the Cathedral. She suddenly became acutely ill and was admitted to a Sydney hospital for an exploratory operation, which revealed advanced cancer of the uterus.

Marion was a woman of great faith in prayer. She understood faith as it is described in the New Testament and she lived it out in her daily life. She had a remarkable ministry of intercession and knew what it was to fast as well as to pray. No doubt her meaningful involvement in these things was a main factor in what was to happen. She asked if the elders of the church would come to the hospital and pray for her healing.

One of the clergy and two lay people went to the hospital, and found her in a long dormitory-type ward. But no sooner had they seated themselves by Marion's bed than a nurse appeared to give her some treatment. Obviously there was to be no time for quiet reflection and leisurely prayer; so they immediately laid hands on her as an outward sign of inward faith and briefly prayed with her: "Thank you, Father, for your promise of healing. We accept this now and believe it for and with Marion. By faith we affirm that she has received the answer to this prayer through Christ our Lord. Amen." She was anointed, and they said the Grace together. They then left, saying they would see her again within the next day or so. It had been a pastoral visit of the briefest possible kind.

A few days later they went to see her again, hoping to be able to spend more time with her. They found her sitting on the side of the bed and she greeted them with a radiant smile. "I have wonderful news. On Tuesday, as soon as our prayer concluded, my body was filled with a burning and vibrating heat which lasted for two hours. I knew that I was being healed! Today, I was taken to the theatre to have radium inserted around the tumour, but the doctors could find no trace of the cancer. They were amazed, and they have told me so."

She was discharged from the hospital without further treatment.

Jane Lambert speaks as one who has been mentally ill — one of those people who has travelled through the deep waters of chronic depression which is one of the most difficult problems a person can have.

"I have heard that most people who commit suicide are suffering from depression," she says. "I can well believe it. One feels closed in by a black cloud which blots out everything else, even when there's no reason for it. You cannot laugh or cry or pray — or even think. All systems are 'stop'. God seems very far away or even not to exist. And the depression gets worse; being depressed makes you more depressed. More and more you want to withdraw within yourself. In this sickness I can well understand how death becomes a welcome solution."

A friend advised Jane to go to the healing service, and

somehow she went. Just for something to do, she continued attending; it gave her some peace — like waves lapping against a boat. But the depression continued.

"One night, in the sermon, something was said that seemed to stand out," Jane continues. "What could I learn from my problem?" "Learn? Nothing," I thought. "I'm miserable and other people just don't understand me."

Then at a later meeting, another challenging thought came: "We should be God-centred, not problem-centred." "That rocked my boat," she says, "because I *was* problem centred."

Now Jane began to listen with new interest. Gradually she picked up the message. Instead of just thinking "I've got a problem," something positive had to be done about it — she had to depend on God more.

"It seemed all right," she said, "but I was like the man with the barrow — I had the job in front of me. But at least I had some idea of what to do — and that was something!"

Jane relates how these thoughts began to penetrate and exercise her mind over a period of months. She tried reaching out to God — and, to her surprise, she found she didn't really want to!

"Sometimes there is a peculiar satisfaction in being sick," she explains. "The sickness becomes a kind of companion and one lives in one's own little world — it saves the effort of having to face the world outside."

It was a long struggle for Jane. She could only live one day at a time, reaching out for God and depending on him just for that day. She would get a thought from her daily reading and concentrate on that. Some books like *God Calling* she found helpful. And she would repeat aloud the promises of Jesus as she claimed them as her own. "All things are possible to him who believes."[2] "My peace I give to you."[3] "I will never forsake you..."[4]

"I still had another lesson to learn," Jane relates. "Not only had I to depend on God for the lifting of my depression — I also had to be changed as a person! The Bible says, 'If anyone is in Christ, he is a new creation; the old has passed away, behold, the new has come.'5 I had thought that being a Christian only meant being forgiven, but now I was learning that it also meant being changed — becoming a different person. Nothing spectacular happened — it was a gradual change. But now in more ways than one I was on a voyage of discovery.

"All this time I continued to think of myself as having depression, mainly because I would have bouts that were as bad as they had ever been. But one day, when I was depressed, I suddenly realised that it was December — and I hadn't been depressed since about June. Before, I had been depressed every few weeks and the attacks had been getting more frequent. Now I had been depressed only once in the last six months. I was being healed!

"I don't remember what happened after that as far as the sickness was concerned. Certainly it still came back at times, often without any cause — depression is like that. But once I could see that the clouds were really breaking and lifting, I took off like a bird. Now I knew for sure that the healing ministry worked — and I knew how to make it work! And now I am perfectly well. I don't think about the terrible times I had; in fact I'm even thankful for them, because without them I would never have learned what I did. Praise God!"

Julia came to the healing service at the Cathedral with a catalogue of problems, emotional and physical, which would daunt the stoutest soul. Bitter of heart from old hurts, limited by long-standing physical ailments, including epilepsy, she had turned to hard drugs and alcohol. She had also been a long-term patient in a psychiatric hospital. But she heard of the service where sick people went for prayer and "decided to give it a go."

"During the service," says Julia, "I went out to the front of the congregation for prayer for my epilepsy. To my great embarrassment I took a fit while kneeling there! I vowed I would never come again."

However, because she was desperate Julia did come back to the service. On the second occasion when others moved to the front for prayer, she stayed firmly in her seat. But one of the congregation, sensing her need, put a hand on her shoulder and said, "Go forward for prayer." She went.

"There in front of the church and in answer to prayer," says Julia, "I felt what I can only describe as something 'snap' inside my head. And, praise God, I have not had an epileptic fit in the seven years since then."

Julia also had a problem of sexual deviation. She asked the leaders to pray over her for healing and they ministered to her with the laying on of hands. During the prayer one of the leaders discerned that the sexual problem was caused by an unclean spirit. He was so overwhelmed by the horribleness of this spirit that he broke down and wept. There followed a ministry of deliverance when they believed that the spirit was being loosed from her in the name of Jesus. She was immediately healed and there has been no recurrence in the years that have gone by.

From that time on Julia went to live with people who were involved in the healing ministry. The loving concern and believing prayer of Christian friends has meant much to her as she has travelled the road to wholeness. It has been a long hard road, not without its failures and setbacks but, supported by her friends, Julia has persevered in prayer. "Let steadfastness have its full effect..."[6]

The end result of the ministry is that Julia has lost her addiction to drugs and her craving for alcohol. She has been delivered from these problems in answer to the continued prayer of faith. And so it is no surprise for her to say, "God has given me a great love for people who can't find an answer to life. I know that Jesus Christ is the only answer, and I want to tell them what Christ can do if only they will surrender to him. What he has done for me he can do for others."

A member of the Healing Ministry Congregation relates this story:

Mrs Stacey arrived in Australia virtually blind — a warm, vivacious, happy person, in spite of her years of sickness and the ultimate gloom which chronic iritis with secondary glaucoma inflicted upon her. She had ventured out from the shores of her homeland with a companion to take her last look at the beauties of this world before the rest of her life was enveloped in the darkness which such diseases can ultimately inflict. But by the time she reached Sydney after some months of travelling, her only remaining visual capacity was the ability to discern night from day.

By God's grace I happened to meet her after the Sunday morning service at St Andrew's Cathedral, and because of her obvious problem I drove her back to her hotel. Moved with concern for her, I shared with her the great truths of God's healing purposes, and related examples of those who could testify to these purposes through the ministry of the Cathedral healing service. This excited faith and hope in her, and she readily agreed to come to the healing service the following Wednesday when she received prayer for her healing.

Mrs Stacey was easily persuaded to cancel her flight from Australia the next day and to remain in Sydney to receive further ministry. As always, she was advised to focus wholly on the promises of God, to hope in his mercies and his sure healings, and to be thankful for healing as it took place. Daily she was encouraged to explore her darkened world for the dawning of new sight, coming from the re-creating power of God's grace. And her search was not in vain, for daily more and more of the world around her was lit up, as she began to see — first shadows, then objects, then colours as day dawned again for her.

When she finally left Australia, she walked out to the aircraft unaided, mounted the stairs with ease and looked back to wave farewell. She radioed from her first stopping place that her healing had further progressed and that she had read two pages of large print. We responded with a cable to her home expressing praise and thanksgiving to God, which she later read herself.

After returning to her home and to her doctors, she wrote to tell us that they could find no remaining signs of either iritis or glaucoma. All the praise and glory belongs to Jesus who is "risen with healing in his wings".

*   *   *

What are we to make of these cases? It is obvious that they are remarkable instances of divine healing. Might it not be that the persons concerned fulfilled the conditions that enabled God to act in this way? If so, what are those conditions? And how can we pray so that our prayers are answered in the same wonderful way?

The promises of God

If we are going to draw on any gift or blessing from God, no matter what it is, our very first requirement is to know what is available to us; the things God wants us to have. We call this God's will. We have to know what God wants to do for us, so that our prayers will be in harmony with his will. This is brought out in part of the prayer that Jesus taught us, "Thy will be done, on earth as it is in heaven."[7]

For God does not act in a capricious way so that we do not know what to expect. In Jesus he has drawn close to us and has made an agreement with us which we call a Testament or Covenant. He has chosen to limit himself to this agreement so that we know he will act in certain ways. These have been revealed to us, primarily by Jesus and recorded for us in the New Testament, which refers to them as "precious and very great promises".[8] This is why we need the scriptures and why we need to "search the scriptures".[9] For it is not just a matter of what we want or what we might work out. It is what God has revealed. So we need to read the Bible to see what God has promised and provided for us.

Now these promises are various. For example, he has promised that if we confess our sins, he can be depended upon to forgive us and to cleanse us from every wrong.[10] So, if we are conscious that we have done what is wrong, either as far as God or as other people are concerned, we can know that if we confess our sins to God, he will forgive us and he will cleanse us. And our assurance of this is nothing less than the promise of God recorded for us in scripture.

Healing by Christ

What, then, are the promises of God about divine healing? We will see the answer to this question more clearly if we first remind ourselves that Jesus, in his earthly ministry, showed again and again that it was his will and practice to heal those who were sick. In fact, almost every page of each of the four gospels contains illustrations of how he did this. These stories differ one from another, but each one makes a distinctive contribution to our understanding. They add up to this: Jesus healed, he always healed, he never failed to heal, and he healed them all.

The story of the healing of Peter's mother-in-law and what happened afterwards is a case in point.[11] She was sick with a high fever and had taken to her bed. When Christ entered the house, everyone called on him to heal her. He went to her bedside and spoke the word of healing, and immediately her temperature returned to normal and she got up and prepared a meal for them. The same evening the surrounding villagers brought everyone who was sick to him and irrespective of what their diseases were, he administered the laying on of hands to them and they were all healed.

There were a number of reasons why Jesus did this, and these are discussed in detail in Part II of this book. For the moment we will refer to two of them. The Bible says that our Lord healed because he felt compassion for people in their need. When the two blind men called out to him, "Lord, let our eyes be opened," we read that "Jesus in pity touched their eyes, and immediately they received their sight and followed him."[12]

Jesus did not even require that people be forgiven beforehand. Certainly he sometimes ministered the forgiveness of sins *before* he laid his hands on them for healing. On other occasions he healed them *first*, then forgave their sins. But very often, he was just content to heal without making any other stipulation at that time. He healed them simply because he loved them and was sensitive to their needs.

Jesus gave another reason for healing when he said, "We must work the works of him who sent me."[13] In other words, healing is what God wants done in the world and it is our responsibility to see it is carried out. Notice how our Lord's statement begins. "*We* must work..." Though this statement is in the context of a healing that Christ himself was about to perform, it shows that healing is an assignment given to others as well as to himself.

Healing by the disciples

That healing was a general assignment is also shown by the fact that Jesus spent much time training his followers to go out and continue what he had begun. "He who believes in me will also do the works that I do,"[14] he told them. So he sent them out to preach the gospel, i.e. the forgiveness of sins, and to heal the sick. The works that the Father had given to him to do became the works that his followers did as well.

The healing ministry of his followers can be seen to perfection in what happened on one occasion when Peter and John were going to church.[15]

When the two disciples arrived at the door of the temple, they saw a man who was crippled. He had been like this all his life and not surprisingly, he was looking for a handout. And Peter said to him, "We haven't any money, but in the name of Jesus, get up and walk." But that was not all.

Having said this to the man, he put his faith into action by taking him by the hand and lifting him up. It was then that his feet and ankles were made strong, and he began to walk and jump and praise God. Naturally this created a sensation, because the people recognised the man as the one who had been crippled and who had lain at the church door. Yet here he was, completely healed through the ministry of those early Christians!

The casual nature of the whole encounter is obvious. There were no special circumstances that brought about the miracle. The man had a need, and in the course of doing something else, the apostles simply stopped by to heal him. If we take the trouble to examine this story, we will find in it the conditions which enable divine healing to take place today and which are discussed throughout the rest of the book.

The healing ministry today

Most of us, of course, are quite used to the idea of Jesus healing the sick. In the same way, we are used to the idea of the first Christians having a healing ministry. But how many of us realise that this is what God is still wanting to do today?

I have to confess that though I have now been a clergyman of the Anglican Church for 30 years, for nearly the first ten of those years I had never really heard of divine healing. Certainly I referred to it occasionally in sermons, but only to explain that it was something that happened a long time ago and was not part of the ministry of the church today.

How strange it is that we take it upon ourselves to make statements like that without a shred of scriptural authority for doing so! For what the Bible actually says about healing today is what is quoted at the beginning of this chapter, James 5: 14,15. As a matter of fact, the *only* instruction given in the New Testament to Christians as to what they are to do when they are sick, is that they are to call the elders of the church. It is, of course, right and good to call the doctor. But the specific thing the Christian is to do is to ask for prayer for healing. And in response, the elders are to pray over him, anointing him with oil, and "the prayer of faith will save the sick man, and the Lord will raise him up."

This is a promise of God which is as clear and definite and uncompromising as any other promise in the New Testament. We can be glad indeed for this provision, but if we are to draw on it effectively we need to understand what it says in some depth. So let us examine the text in more detail.

Do the sick need faith?

"Is any among you sick? Let him call for the elders of the church." It is quite clear from this instruction that the person who is sick has got to do something. He has to call. He has to have enough faith to ask that the faith of other Christians be shared with him.

In this ministry I have found that whenever I have initiated the contact with someone in need, simply because he was in need, my prayer has seldom been effective. Indeed, so much has this been so, that now I would not approach anyone and offer to pray the prayer of faith for his or her healing. Instead I would do what I am doing in this chapter — explain the promise of God to him and what he must do. When the sick person understands the resource that is available and takes the initiative in asking for prayer, I find that the relationship is always fruitful because of the faith he has shown in taking that step.

The responsibility of the church

The faith that is shared with the person wanting to draw on healing is the faith of the church. It is not just the faith of the one who is sick, though, as we have seen, he needs to have faith enough to call. Again, it is not just the faith of the minister or the priest. He is only one part of the church. It is the faith of the lay people and the clergy together, for they are the church. The elders of the church represent the whole body of believers, and so it is the faith of everyone that is drawn upon and used. This means that all members of the church must know what to do and how to do it if the person who is sick is to be effectively ministered to.

I was once described as a "Faith Healer". I didn't agree with that description. I tried to explain that it is *God* who heals and that it is the faith of the *church* that is important. And that is what is being said in this chapter. We must know the promise of God to heal; the person who is sick must have faith to come and ask; and the faith of the church must be added to his faith that he may receive the healing he needs.

Praying in faith

The kind of praying the church is to do is called the prayer of faith. It is most important that we understand what is meant by this, and that we follow it through in the right way.

A young Christian man once came to me for healing. He had fallen on a wet concrete floor at the factory where he worked, seriously injuring his back, and it had not so far responded to medical treatment. He said that he had prayed about it, but when I asked him how he prayed, he replied, rather defensively, "Well, I was sincere." I said that I was glad he was sincere, but that it wasn't *just* sincerity that enabled God's blessing to come to us.

It just isn't enough for our prayers to have other good and necessary characteristics if they do not express faith as it is described in the Scriptures. We will be examining this in much greater length later on. In fact it is so important for us to learn to pray the prayer of faith in the right way that the next chapter is devoted entirely to this subject. Sufficient for the moment to say faith in prayer means that you believe you have received the answer to your prayer to the point where you do not doubt in your heart.[16]

Once, after I had been speaking at a church about the prayer of faith, one of the church wardens came to me and commented, "We don't so much as think our prayers are going to be answered. We open our mouths to God and out come mere words." I agree with him. Except in one area (which we will refer to later) the prayer of faith in the church, in my view, is a dead letter.

Someone has said that the greatest thing in the world is not prayer — it is *answered* prayer. This book affirms throughout that if our prayers are going to be answered, if the promises of God are going to become real in our lives, and if we are going to be "raised up", then we must pray in the way that God has shown us. And the Bible calls this way "the prayer of faith".[17]

Progressive healing

There is one thing more that needs to be said about divine healing generally before we look at it in more detail in the following chapters. It is this: only a minority of people are healed at once. The majority of those who are healed find that their healing is progressive. Jesus said that according to our faith, or in proportion to our faith, so our prayers would be answered.

Of course, if our faith is equal to the mountain of sickness to be moved, there is no reason why our prayer cannot be answered at once. But as we all realise, the church is only now in the process of recovering its ministry of healing. So very often it has hardly been heard of, let alone practised, and not infrequently it is opposed.

In many cases, too, when people finally come for divine healing, their sickness is very advanced. In fact, this is often *why* they come. They have exhausted all other possibilities, and they turn to divine healing as a last resort. No criticism of them is intended here — that is not the point. But we have to be realistic and face the facts as they are.

This means that very often our faith is *small* and the mountain is *big*. But for our very great encouragement, we need to know that if our faith is not equal to the task immediately, it does not mean that we are not going to be healed. It means rather that our healing is more likely to come progressively.

The Bible makes this clear when it links healing with the kingdom of God. Jesus said that healing is part of a greater reality called the kingdom of God, and that it is the character of the kingdom to grow, "first the blade, then the ear, then the full grain in the ear".[18] This means that where our faith is small and the mountain is big, we can think of our healing coming to us like the growing of a plant. Again, we will enlarge on this principle as we go along.

To summarise what we have been thinking about in this first chapter:

> To begin with, we have to know what the promises of God are, because his promises reveal his will. His will is shown in what Christ did, in what Christ commissioned his followers to do, and in the promises he has made to us.

> If the sick person has not enough faith to believe for himself, he needs to have faith enough to call on the church to pray with him. The prayer that is prayed is the prayer of faith.

> And not least, we need to know that if the healing is not there at once, it can come progressively.

Christ heals today in the same way as he healed in the days of his earthly ministry, because he is the same today as he was yesterday. But now he uses our faith, yours and mine. There is no limit to what God can do — as our case histories have shown — if we know what is available and how to draw on it effectively.

A Prayer

Loving Father in Heaven, I come to you as one who would understand your will more perfectly. I confess that I have not thought about these things as much as I should and have taken many things for granted. I have been reading your Word not thinking of healing as being something that can be drawn on today. I know that in this way I have limited the blessing that you would give me, and that I have limited the blessing I could have given to others.

I ask now that you will use my reading of this book so that the Holy Spirit will show me what I should understand about divine healing. I ask that you will enlighten my reading of the scriptures so that you reveal yourself and your truth to me. I ask this so that I will be a better child of God and a more meaningful servant of yours in the world.

Thank you now for the answers to this prayer that you will give me. Through Christ our Lord.

2

The Prayer of Faith

Now faith is the assurance of things hoped for, the conviction of things not seen.   Hebrews 11: 1

As they passed by in the morning, they saw the fig tree withered away to its roots. And Peter remembered and said to him, "Master, look! The fig tree which you cursed has withered." And Jesus answered them, "Have faith in God. Truly, I say to you, whoever says to this mountain, 'Be taken up and cast into the sea,' and does not doubt in his heart, but believes that what he says will come to pass, it will be done for him. Therefore I tell you, whatever you ask in prayer, believe that you have received it, and it will be yours."   Mark 11: 20-24

Let him ask in faith, with no doubting.   James 1:6

IN THE PREVIOUS chapter we referred to the great promises that are contained in James ch. 5: "The prayer of faith will save the sick man, and the Lord will raise him up; and if he has committed sins, he will be forgiven." As well as giving this series of promises, James gives the further information that they are made effective through *the prayer of faith*. This means that, as well as being concerned with what God promises, we need also to be concerned with what *we have to do* to appropriate these promises. Both are necessary; without God man cannot, without man God will not. In this chapter therefore we are going to concentrate on *our part* and what *we* are to do.

What is the prayer of faith?

From the time that the ministry of divine healing first began to be exercised in St Andrew's Cathedral in 1960, people have been coming and asking, "What is the prayer of faith?" I wonder what you would say in answer to this question? What, indeed, is the prayer of faith? It isn't much good using an expression unless we have a clear understanding of what it means. We will find an explanation from Jesus himself in the passage quoted at the beginning of this chapter.

You may remember that just before this, Jesus had done a most unlikely thing. He had cursed a fig tree. Why he did this need not concern us here; the fact is that he did. And when our Lord and his disciples came by next day, Peter noticed that the tree was already dead. He commented on it, and Jesus then used the incident to illustrate what is meant by faith in prayer. Turning to his followers, he said, "Have faith in God... Whoever says to this mountain, 'Be taken up and cast into the sea,' and does not doubt in his heart, but believes...it will be done for him. Therefore I tell you, whatever you ask in prayer, believe that you have received it, and it will be yours."

Jesus is saying here that if prayer is to be answered, then we have to believe our prayer is *being* answered. His original words really mean, "believe that you *have received* it;" not "'might receive," or "will receive," or even "are receiving," but "have received." We are to believe the prayer has been answered; it is an accomplished fact. To make it abundantly clear, Jesus said that this belief is to be to the point where *we do not doubt in our heart*. He leaves no room for uncertainty or compromise on the matter. We are to believe the answer has been received so that we have no doubt or reservation at all.

When we read in the New Testament about faith for healing, either in the ministry of Christ, or of the disciples, or of our need of faith, this is what is meant. And when Jesus said that if we have faith as a grain of mustard seed, he meant that we need only to have this certainty in the most minute form, for there to be blessing. (This does not leave out the quantitative aspect of faith that we will refer to elsewhere.)

This certainty applies not only to prayer about healing. In fact healing is not even mentioned in this particular passage. Jesus says rather, "*whatever* you ask in prayer..." It applies to healing, because it is the prayer of faith that will raise up the sick man. It applies to everything else, because that is how we are *always* to pray if our prayers are to be effective.

Let it be crystal clear that if our prayer, whether it be for healing or anything else, is going to be answered by Almighty God, then we have to pray in the way he has revealed to us through Jesus. For with God there is no variableness or shadow of turning. God does not change to suit us; we have to change to suit him. This is another reason why we need to search the scriptures; to see how we are to respond to our heavenly Father. Our need and our responsibility is that we understand how we are to pray. It is fundamental and central to us having any and all of God's blessings in our life and ministry.

So the first point for us to note about the prayer of faith is that we must know what God has promised to give us. The second, and present point, is that we are to believe that we receive these promises so that we have no doubt in our heart.

What are your prayers like?

Do your prayers express belief that God is answering them so that you are sure? Sometimes it is a very useful exercise to have what we call "a prayer laboratory". In this group activity we ask for someone who has a genuine need to allow the other Christians who are there to pray for him. This brother explains his particular need and the others gather around and lay hands on him and pray the prayer of faith with him and for him.

After several people have prayed, we have a discussion about the prayers that have been offered. The idea is to take note of the strong points in the prayers — where faith has been expressed in the way that Jesus taught. Then we comment in a kind but candid way about the weaknesses, which will be where the prayers have been expressed differently from the way Jesus taught. When we are enabled to look at our praying in this objective way, we realise, perhaps for the first time, how often we fail to measure up to the kind of prayer we ought to be engaging in constantly — the prayer that believes a promise of God is being received in our real-life situation.

Do *you* pray the prayer of faith? This is the question that I hope you are asking yourself at this stage. Because it is not enough for your prayers to have other commendable features; it makes no difference who you are or what denomination you belong to; it doesn't matter whether you are a new Christian or you are one who has known the Lord all your life; if your prayers are going to be answered by God, you have to *believe* they are being answered so that you do not doubt. This fact cannot be over-emphasised.

We believe this by faith. A Church Army officer once said to me, "Faith means that you're thanking God *before* it happens." This insight is exactly what we must understand at this point. It echoes those words in the Epistle to the Hebrews, "Faith is the assurance of things hoped for, the conviction of things not seen." Jesus said the same thing: "Blessed are those who have not seen and yet believe."[1]

Faith is not what we see. Faith always goes beyond what we see to what we hope for and to what we believe we receive. That is why we thank God for the answer to our prayer *before* the answer is seen. When it is seen, we thank him by sight — but then we are no longer thanking him by faith. And it is the *prayer of faith* that we are concerned about here, not just for healing, but for any promise of God that we are drawing on.

We will understand this better if we relate it to an area of prayer which is already familiar to us, and where we usually "get it right." This will give us guidelines as to how to act out faith in prayer in those areas where at present we do *not* "get it right." The area to which I want to refer is the experience of conversion.

The prayer of faith for conversion

We can thank God that in the church generally there is some clarity of understanding and effectiveness of practice on the matter of conversion. This is the area of prayer where faith is understood as it should be. If we see how the prayer of faith is exercised in conversion, we will more easily see the point I am seeking to make about the prayer of faith in general.

If a person wants to become a Christian, he must first realise that he is without Christ in his life. We are either in Christ or we are not; we are either lost or we are found; we are either born again or we are "dead through trespasses and sins,"[2] to use scriptural language. The first requirement is for the person to know that he *needs* to be converted.

The second thing to know is that God has made him a precious and very great promise — that if he believes on Christ in repentance, faith and obedience, he will be saved. The gaoler at Philippi said to Paul in prison, "What must I do to be saved?" And Paul replied, "Believe in the Lord Jesus, and you will be saved,"[3] meaning, "Put your trust in him as your Saviour and Lord."

The third thing is that the intending convert must believe in Christ for himself. Different people may act on this in different ways, but there is a word that expresses what every convert does at this point; he *accepts* Christ. He comes to the point where he makes up his mind; he makes a decision. And so he responds to the promise of God and consciously accepts Christ as the one who saves him. The surer he is that he has done this, the more easily he will enter into the reality of conversion.

What happens at this point can be illustrated quite simply. I might say to the person concerned, "If I want to give you my watch as a gift, what have you to do for it to be yours?" I want him to see that all he has to do is to accept it, so I get him to take it from my hand. And as he holds the watch, he becomes accustomed to the idea that he has accepted it, and that it is now his. He must accept Christ in the same definite way.

When he has done this, I go on and say to him that he may find his life changed at the time — and if it is, that is fine. But if it isn't he must on no account rely on his feelings. If he is not changed at once, it does not mean that nothing has happened. It means that his faith is being tested and that he must continue to affirm that he has accepted Christ — by faith.

Let me illustrate this from my own experience. As a late teenager, I first believed in Christ at an evangelistic mission conducted by the Reverend (now Canon) H.M. Arrowsmith. We were invited to raise our hands as an outward sign that we were accepting Christ, And that is what I did. We were then asked to wait behind and the missioner shook hands with each of us. I will always remember him asking me, "Are you sure you have accepted Christ?" I told him that I had.

At that time I had no religious or church background that would give an adequate understanding of the commitment I was making. Perhaps that was the explanation for what subsequently happened, or what *didn't* happen, because for three years after I had accepted Christ as my Saviour, I neither felt nor saw any difference in my life — nothing at all. I just held on by faith to what I believed had happened. Only as those years went by, and very gradually, did I come to experience the Spirit of God at work in my life.

But isn't this what faith is all about? If a person who has accepted Christ does not experience a change in his life straight away, we help him to understand, we call on him to affirm, that he has accepted Christ *by faith*. And if he were to say, "Oh! I accepted Christ, but nothing has happened," we would conclude that he had not reached the point where he understood faith and was exercising it. For when we exercise faith, we are thanking God for what we have asked of him, even though *we do not see it at the time*. It is most important that we understand this clearly.

The point we are making here is that in conversion we are praying the prayer of faith. To use the language in Mark, chapter 11, we believe that we have received Christ, and we believe to the point where we do not doubt in our heart. To use the language that is in more common use, we accept Christ, and we continue to affirm this by faith. The advantage of this second way of expressing it is that it puts into simple and effective words what we need to know and do if the blessing is to be ours. But let us realise that what we are really talking about is the prayer of faith.

My suggestion at this stage is that you spend time thinking this out for yourself. I spend a lot of my own time in what I call "prayer-thinking" — just sorting out the things of faith in my mind so that I get them right. Sometimes I do this during my daily prayer time, sometimes while I am going for a walk — preferably on my own. I spend this time just "nutting it out" — putting it all into a consistent whole, following it through to its logical conclusion and applying it in real-life situations.

A clergyman friend once said to me, "I get the prayer of faith right when it comes to conversion, but I don't seem to get it right at other times." I replied to him, "Well it is about time we *all* got it right at *other* times." Let us now do that as far as we are concerned by applying to divine healing what we have learned about the prayer of faith in conversion.

The prayer of faith for healing

When someone comes to me wishing to draw upon divine healing, I often ask him if he is a Christian. If he is, I remind him of how he prayed the prayer of faith at his conversion and explain that this is the way we are going to pray the prayer of faith for his healing. Of course, we first talk over the particular problems he has, so that ministry can be offered to him in the most relevant way. But sooner or later we reach the point where we want to appropriate God's promise that the prayer of faith will save the sick man and that the Lord will raise him up.

I will then pray for that person something like this: "Our loving Father, we come to you in the name of Jesus Christ our Lord for this your servant who has a need for healing. We thank you that you have made a promise in your word to raise him up so that his need is met. We now pray the prayer of faith so that your promise is made effective in full and blessed reality in his life. Father, we now accept your promise of healing for him and with him. We believe that he receives this blessing so that we do not doubt in our heart. By faith we affirm that you are now raising him up. For the blessings that we will see at once, we thank you by sight, and for those blessings that we do not see at once, we thank you by faith. But whether it be by sight or by faith, we praise your name through Christ. Amen."

Then I say to him, "Now you pray the prayer of faith." It is good to pray for people, but when all is said and done, that is only to enable them to reach the point of being able to pray for themselves. So I ask the person to pray the prayer of faith himself. I encourage him and try to help him feel at ease. I tell him to accept God's healing for himself and I help him with his prayer if necessary. And so, with or without assistance, the person does for himself what I have already done on his behalf.

I am thankful that most people are able to accept divine healing for themselves in a way that is real to them, especially if the principles of the prayer of faith have been explained to them carefully. But it is astonishing how difficult it is for some people — and they are usually the habitual, set-in-their-ways type of church people — to make a simple acceptance of God's blessings, so that they are thanking him by faith. Instead they use a lot of religious language which, when it is all added up, means very little as far as faith is concerned. They are the most difficult folk to assist.

Assuming the prayer of faith has been worked through with the sick person, I then explain what should happen as a result. I say something like this: "When you were converted, you might have been changed in a moment, or you might have felt no difference at all. Most people feel nothing at first, but they are not put off by this. Rather they learn to thank God by faith. Now this time we have prayed the prayer of faith for healing. If you are healed at once, praise God! You will be praising him by sight! But you might find, especially where the mountain of illness is big and our faith is small, that there is no outward change at first. You have prayed the prayer of faith, and I, representing the elders of the church, have prayed the prayer of faith. But this is where our faith is tested. This is where we affirm that you *are* being healed — by faith! As in conversion, so in healing."

But what actually happens with healing in so many cases is that the person says in effect: "I prayed the prayer of faith, *but* I am not healed." You can see that if we applied this to conversion, the person would never enter into an assurance of salvation. And so with healing; the person concerned must realise that praying the prayer of faith means thanking God and continuing to thank God by faith, believing that he is answering the prayer. Faith does not say, "Yes...but..." Faith says, "Yes... Praise God, Praise God." Or as somebody has facetiously put it — there are two sorts of people, the sheep and the goats; and the goats "but"!

Let us now look at these principles in some real-life situations.

The painful back

A colleague, the Reverend Harry Broadhurst, had bouts of recurring backache. At first the condition had been diagnosed as muscular rheumatism, but as time passed it became obvious that the condition was more serious and was progressively worsening. He sought the advice of a specialist, who told him that he had a type of arthritis of the spine which was due to degenerative changes in both the bones and the cartilages in the vertebral column. As the condition would be progressive, the specialist advised surgery in order to immobilise the lower spine at the two affected levels. Harry was told that without surgery he could become a spinal cripple.

Harry continues the story himself: "I prayed for the healing of my body, but I realised that I had only a mental acceptance that God was able to heal. While listening to a sermon on prayer and fasting for healing, the Lord seemed to be telling me that fasting would be necessary in my case also. I decided immediately that I would take nothing but water until such time as the Lord would deal with me. Three and a half days later, while praying with the elders of the church, I was filled with the Holy Spirit, and had a complete heart acceptance of my healing.

"The next morning the pain in my back was as intense as ever, but this did not daunt my new faith. All my thoughts seemed to be focusing on the unseen rather than on the seen. The pain continued for ten whole days, but my faith did not falter. I knew that I was healed, for God had spoken! On the eleventh morning I awoke to discover the pain gone! Subsequent medical examination revealed that there was now no need for an operation."

That occurred twenty years ago. Recently I asked Harry if the healing had continued. He assured me that the healing had been perfect in all this time.

The migraine sufferer

A university lecturer and his wife, Roger and Carol Peterson, came to see me because Carol was a chronic migraine sufferer, and the attacks were becoming progressively worse. After we had worked through the matter, we reached the point where we prayed the prayer of faith and I accepted healing for her. They both understood what I had done, and they too accepted healing on her account.

Some weeks later when I next saw Roger, I asked about his wife. He told me, with typical male brevity, that following our time of prayer Carol had not had another migraine. Later I had the chance to speak to Carol myself — and she gave me the full details.

For some time after we had all prayed the prayer of faith and had accepted healing on her behalf she was free from her complaint, but the time came when she felt the early symptoms of an attack coming on. Previously, whenever these symptoms had appeared, she had taken her medication and gone to bed and been really ill for several days. But this time she straightway declared, "Lord I have accepted your healing and I now affirm it by faith. I will not let you go until you bless me by sight." She continued to express in positive statements what she had accepted by faith until the headache lessened and finally went away. It did not become a true migraine.

Later she was threatened with another attack. She could easily have said to herself, "I must be reasonable about all this — I do have a headache, I'll take my medication and lie down." No one would have blamed her for doing that, but if she had given in to the symptoms she *would* have had a migraine, and she would not have been healed. But Carol now knew what she must do, and straightway — almost as an automatic reaction — she began to affirm, "Lord, I have accepted your healing and I continue to affirm it by faith so that it will become what I have by sight. Thank you Father in Jesus' name."

The point about the continued affirmations is that they enabled her to believe so that she did not doubt in her heart. And again the symptoms decreased without taking over. Whenever the attacks of migraine threatened with all their usual frightening symptoms, Carol held on by faith to the firm belief in her healing. Gradually she found the attacks became less frequent and less severe, and eventually she came to a level of experience where the migraine was a thing of the past — and it has never recurred.

A gradual healing

Earlier we referred to Marion Summers, who had a cancer and was immediately healed. Here now we have a case which took longer.

Joyce Atkinson had a mole on her right arm which began to grow and bleed. Medical specialists diagnosed it as melanoma and advised the amputation of her arm. Even so, they said this would give no assurance of healing. Joyce and her husband Robert decided against the amputation, and prayed the prayer of faith for healing. They were both informed Christians and knew what it was to exercise faith for healing. They accepted healing so that it was *what* they accepted — by faith.

Joyce was no better at first; indeed her condition continued to deteriorate. But they believed they were drawing on a promise of God and they thanked God so that they did not doubt. This meant that they continued to affirm healing by faith until the pain and distress fell away. It was anything but easy. It took discipline of mind to react to the difficulties in that way and to do it consistently.

The nights were the worst. They would just "walk the floor" affirming what they were believing by faith until it became what they had by sight. As they continued in this way, the intervals between the attacks of pain increased and relief from it became easier to draw on. After some nine months of affirming healing by faith in this way, the symptoms finally disappeared completely. Joyce has since been cleared by her medical advisers and continues in perfect health.

The recurrent hernia

Paul Lindquist is a clinical psychologist by profession, and a sincere Christian with a commitment to the healing ministry. He had an operation for an inguinal hernia in 1972 but some time later the hernia recurred. Lifting even moderate weights caused discomfort and sudden stooping could be quite uncomfortable. These symp-- toms grew worse as the hernia redeveloped until even the movements associated with ordinary walking caused him distress.

Early in 1976, Paul sought medical advice and was told what he expected to be told; that the repair had broken down and that he would have to undergo further surgery. But Paul had a conviction that God would heal him in response to faith and he continued to exercise faith to that end. About the middle of 1976 he attended a service of divine healing and sought the laying on of hands. He had prepared himself through repentance and faith, and believed that, through the laying on of hands, the Saviour's healing would be given.

He describes in his own words what happened. "I came away from the service knowing that the symptoms were still present. I realised that it was necessary for me to continue to believe Christ's healing and not my symptoms. After about three days of on-going faith I became aware that the symptoms were disappearing. I was walking without any discomfort and also found that I could even jump without pain. I began to leap with joy and my whole being seemed to be filled with his praise. I walked 8-10 km. to my office, rejoicing in my healing and in the fellowship I had with Jesus.

"Lifting, digging, swimming and running have now become commonplace. With it all I am constantly aware of God's desire that I go beyond the first principles of Christianity and be sanctified through and through. I believe that I have been healed so that I might serve him more fully."

Healed to serve

Ted Brooker's problem became evident in 1958, when he was in the army. One side of his face became extremely painful, though it was quite insensitive to touch or to light pin-pricking. A neurophysician diagnosed the condition as syringobulbia, a degenerative condition which affects the upper part of the spinal cord and the brain stem, which join at the base of the skull. The disease is a progressive and incurable condition which brings about changes in sensation to the face and arm with weakness of the muscles involved.

Ted's facial symptoms were accompanied by dizziness and nausea. Deep X-Ray therapy and other treatment gave only temporary relief; and surgery was suggested with the idea of severing a nerve at the base of the brain in order to relieve the pain. By 1967 Ted's condition had so deteriorated that he had to consider giving up work. A visiting specialist from the United States confirmed the diagnosis and said that no medical or surgical treatment could further help him.

About that time someone told Ted's wife of the healing service at the Cathedral, and together they came. Ted had a number of interviews with me; he received the laying on of hands and was anointed; but there was no healing. This led to a crisis in Ted's life, and he was convicted that he was expecting something from God but was doing nothing to appropriate it.

Ted takes up the story: "At our next interview Jim Glennon took off his watch and offered it to me saying, 'Go on, take it.' When I reached out and took it, he said, 'Now, what do you say?' I replied, 'Thank you.' He went on, 'Well, the Lord is offering healing to you — reach out and take it and then say "Thank you!"' And this is what I really did. As a result I began to feel that everything was becoming new.

"Afterwards, Jim invited me to come up to the Bell Tower and watch the bells being rung at the weekly practice. I hadn't told him that I could never go round in circles without experiencing nausea and giddiness, and the way up to the ringing chamber was by a spiral staircase. But I didn't feel nauseated nor did I fall over! I realised then that I *was* being healed!"

The symptoms of the disease quickly disappeared and exhaustive medical tests revealed no trace of the problem. Ted was now described as being "perfectly physically fit."

As a result of this wonderful healing both Ted and Joyce decided to give their lives to the service of God. It wasn't easy; it meant leaving behind their own home and a secure position for a long grind in Bible College with no assured income. They went to the Adelaide Bible Institute and there followed three years of study with God providing for their material needs in extraordinary ways. The Healing Ministry Congregation was privileged to share in this.

After Ted graduated from the A.B.I., he and Joyce went out as missionaries with the Church Missionary Society to our Aboriginal people in the Northern Territory of Australia. After two years there, Ted, who is a Presbyterian, felt called to the full time ministry of his church and this has led to four years further training. At the time of writing he is in his final year and is looking forward to ordination.

This remarkable story of healing is equalled by the Brookers' continued dedication to the cause of Christ. And this is not exceptional. I know of at least twelve young men and women who have entered Bible or Theological College to train for full-time ministry as a result of blessing they have received in St Andrew's Cathedral healing service.

* * *

These testimonies are examples of the prayer of faith in action. Those concerned thought of themselves not in terms of what they saw, but in terms of what they had accepted by faith. For we are to "walk by faith, not by sight."[4] We saw in our analogy with conversion that when a person consciously accepts Christ as Saviour, he is saying in effect, "I know by faith that I am saved." Similarly, when we consciously accept healing, we then say, "I know by faith that I am healed. This is what I accept. Thank you Father in Jesus' name."

Let us summarise what we have said:

We must first know what God has promised to give us. We then appropriate those promises by faith. Faith believes that we have received these things so that we do not doubt.

Our experience of conversion shows how this is followed through in practice — we accept Christ and we affirm it by faith until we experience it in fact.

So too, with healing. We accept it and we continue to thank God by faith until it becomes what we have by sight. But we are only ever able to thank God by sight because we first of all thanked him by faith.

A prayer for healing

Loving Father, we praise your name that you have drawn close to us in Jesus Christ and revealed what you have provided for us and want us to have from your hand. Thank you for your promise to us that the prayer of faith will enable the sick person to be restored to health.

We praise you that you have also revealed to us how we are to pray. Father, forgive us that so very often we have not prayed in the way that Jesus taught us. We would repent of that, and by your grace, so pray that your blessing may be given to us now and at all times.

Father God, I now accept your healing for my need. I accept it humbly and gratefully and completely. I accept it so that it is what I accept and the way I think of myself. I thank you for it and rejoice that I am giving glory to you by exercising faith. I thank you now and will continue to thank you until faith gives way to sight.

Show me what I can do to put my faith into action. As my faith is small, I know you will not expect me to act upon my faith all at once, but I believe you are showing me the first step I am to take.

Through Christ our Lord, Amen.

A final word of guidance

There is one thing more that perhaps needs be said to give

balance and perspective to praying in faith. As faith is what *we* are responsible for, we need to realise our limitations. If we are beginners, we need to put our faith into action in a *beginning* way and choose subjects for prayer that lie within our limited faith experience. As we become more fluent in having faith, we will be able to pray for the removal of mountains that are bigger. But even when we are comparatively experienced, we will still need to recognise our limitations and know when we can pray in faith and when we can only relinquish the matter to God. There is no limit to what God can do, but there *is* a limit to what his servants can do — and wisdom is knowing the difference.

The following points might be kept in mind in making an assessment of what we can do, or not do, when praying for healing.

The more long-standing the problem or the more advanced the sickness, the more difficult it is to do anything effective about it.

If the disease is, humanly speaking, lethal, and especially if this is the dimension that is accepted by the sick person and/or those nearest him, this has to be very much taken into account.

If the disease eg. poliomyelitis, has burnt itself out and the bodily frame has been seriously affected, this is a big mountain to move.

I do not consider it reasonable to believe that an amputee grow a new limb or things like that.

Having said this (and more could be said), the point must always be made that we will go as far as our faith will take us. "All things are possible to him who believes,"[5] Jesus said. But he also said, "According to your faith be it done to you;"[6] and this latter is our present point. Perhaps the only safe and balanced position is for us all to think of ourselves as those who are *learning* how to pray in faith. We might then say: how can my faith grow? Well, that is what the next chapter is all about.

3

How to Increase in Faith

Whenever you stand praying, forgive, if you have anything against anyone; so that your Father also who is in heaven may forgive you your trespasses. Mark 11:25

Love casts out fear. 1 John 4:18

Jesus said, "What is the kingdom of God like? And to what shall I compare it? It is like a grain of mustard seed which a man took and sowed in his garden; and it grew and became a tree, and the birds of the air made nests in its branches." Luke 13: 18,19

WE NOW UNDERSTAND what the prayer of faith is. We are eager to put it to use, and to pray this way for our own needs as well as for the needs of others. But, so often, we are discouraged by the weakness and inadequacy of our faith. Sometimes, it seems, that all the faith we can muster couldn't move an ant hill, let alone a mountain! What has been said about knowing our limitations adds to our concern. How then do we *increase* in faith? What steps can we take to nourish the tender plant of faith within us?

If we search the scriptures, we will find many truths that will help us. Some are positive in nature, and we deal with them, or some of them, in this chapter. Some are negative in the sense that we are told to avoid them. Yet it will be quickly seen that they too are positive, in the sense that they require us to change our way of thinking so that we leave behind our negative and destructive attitudes. We will deal with the negative side first, so that we can then go on and bring into focus the positive things that God wants us to know and to do — that we might increase in faith.

We have to forgive

The first of the passages quoted follows straight on from the one quoted at the beginning of Chapter 2, in which Jesus explained the meaning of faith in prayer. In this present verse he goes on to say that whenever we pray, we must forgive. We must forgive anyone for anything that stands between us and them. The immediate reason given is "so that your Father also who is in heaven may forgive you your trespasses." This is worth pausing over. The same thing is said in the sermon on the mount, and it is also the point in the parable of the unforgiving servant. (Matthew 18: 21-35)

Do we realise that the forgiveness of our own sin, which is another way of referring to our eternal salvation, depends on the reality of our having forgiven everyone for every wrong that has been done to us? "Forgive...that your Father...may forgive you."[1] This doesn't mean that we are forgiven *because* we forgive others. We are forgiven because we believe in Christ for our forgiveness. But if our faith in Christ is to be acceptable to the Father, it must issue in doing the will of God in our life. And that means, in part, that we must forgive others in the same way as we need to be forgiven, by them and by God. We are not saved *because* we forgive others, but we are not saved *unless* we forgive others.

The context also shows that it has an intimate connection with the question of our prayers being answered. A moment's reflection will lead us to see that if we are in a state of being unforgiven and therefore separated from God, then our prayers are not likely to rise any further than the ceiling! This may well explain why many of our prayers remain unanswered.

Now the devil of unforgiveness, and I choose my words carefully, is that it is so often justified. When we need to forgive someone, it is often because that person has taken advantage of us in some way and we have reacted with "righteous indignation." The hurt might involve more than one occasion — indeed, the thing we really need to forgive might be the sum total of a whole series of events. This of course makes it all the more difficult.

We all develop resentments against others at times. Sometimes I become resentful with people for no more reason than that they are sick and are unable to exercise faith for themselves. Despite my efforts to explain the prayer of faith to them and to help them pray for themselves, they remain in bondage to their difficulties. Then I get hung-up on their hang-up!

I have to go on and say I have found in practice that as long as I have any hang-up in my heart and mind about the person for whom I am praying; as long as I retain any degree of resentment or unforgiveness, he or she is never healed. If I am to pray for people effectively, I have to come to the point where I have true oneness with them with no reservation of any kind. I make this statement most seriously.

This need for forgiveness concerns not only the person for whom we are praying; it concerns *anything* we have against *anyone*! It can be difficult enough to have oneness with the person for whom we are praying, let alone have oneness with everyone. But this is what we *have* to do if our prayer is to be answered. And not only about prayer for healing; it applies to prayer about *anything* at all — "whatever you ask in prayer..."[2]

Our Lord is a hard taskmaster in some respects; he does not modify his standpoint because of our weakness. Forgiving other people is something we all have to face if we are going to pray the prayer of faith. We cannot have the slightest disharmony in our relationships, either with one another or with those to whom we minister — or indeed with any other person, alive or dead.

We learn by our mistakes

Let me tell you a story about myself. On one hand it is a confession; on the other I learnt from it, so the end result was good. (A good deal of what I know has come out of my mistakes and failures.)

I once ministered to a man — an architect, who was a chronic depressive. A life-time of business worries had left him almost a mental wreck. He very much wanted me to minister to him, so I regularly went to his home and prayed the prayer of faith with him for his healing. Whenever I prayed with him, he would ask his wife to come in and share the prayer with him. This was a good and happy idea and I welcomed it. But there was a problem — the wife did not welcome my ministry and while she was outwardly accommodating, I knew she talked about it in a destructive way with other people.

I was human enough to resent this, and it meant that whenever I thought of his wife, I reacted in an unforgiving way. As far as healing was concerned, the man made little or no progress, despite my best efforts on his behalf. One day, when I was speaking to him on the telephone and felt his acute distress coming through in the conversation, I suddenly became convicted about the resentment I had towards his wife. I realised that because they were one in marriage, it was just as though I had a resentment against him!

I knew that I had to make this matter right in my own mind and heart, and so I did. It is amazing what one can do when one *has* to; yet one *chooses* to. From then on I disciplined myself to think of his wife only in terms of full Christian acceptance. My ministry with him continued in exactly the same way as it had up to then. But *from the time I forgave his wife*, he began to improve. This he continued to do until he resumed his full place in the community.

Is there any barrier like this in your own life? Is God convicting *you* of your need to forgive someone? If he is, you may be quite sure that he will not let you go until you have put it right. You will not have his peace or answer to prayer, until you have confessed it and entered into reconciliation with the person concerned. "Whenever you stand praying, forgive, if you have anything against anyone."[3]

The problem of fear

The other negative matter which I want to discuss before going on to the positive things we must do, is also of vital importance to us if our faith is to increase. It is something that is diametrically opposed to faith. It is fear.

There are various things that can be said about fear and most of us would be able to contribute something to that understanding. But I wonder how many of us realise that just as faith brings about what we have faith in, so fear brings about what we fear. In the Old Testament, we find Job saying, "The thing that I fear comes upon me, and what I dread befalls me."[4]

Isn't it often true that the very thing we fear most comes to pass? Even in little things? For instance, we sometimes joke that if we are hoping for something, we must expect the opposite. The weather is a common example. If we want a fine day for some special reason, we rather expect that it will turn out to be wet. The real point is that we are *afraid* it is going to be wet. "It's always the way," we then say, which expresses our negative thinking in general.

And in bigger things. Often in my own life something has happened right in front of me, so that I have exclaimed, "That was the very thing I was afraid would happen!" I realise now that I brought it about by my continuing fear thoughts. Whether we know it or not, or like it or not, many of our difficulties come because we believe they will come. We think we are hoping for the best, but in reality we are fearing the worst.

I was once asked to minister to a girl who had cancer, and who died. On the day of her death I was making a pastoral visit to the home when the girl's aunt came in, and said, "We prayed for a miracle, but *the inevitable had to happen.*" I am not being critical; but we have to face the fact, that often we have, or try to have, an outward appearance of faith, but what really grips us is inward fear. And we believe that we have received what we fear so that we do not doubt in our heart!

In passing, that is one reason why it is so difficult to minister divine healing to someone who has cancer. It is because the patient is deeply afraid, and so are his family and friends. I am not saying that fear is the only thing to be concerned about, but I am saying that it is much more the point of concern than we commonly realise. Father John Hope, who was the pathfinder of the healing ministry in Australia, said that he had never known anyone to be healed who was afraid he would *not* be healed.

We must realise that faith and fear are opposed to one another. If faith is to be effective, one has to believe so that one does not doubt. As we have seen, fear believes that what is *feared* is going to happen. Fear therefore negates faith — and having done that, continues on its destructive way.

It will help if we see (in an over-simplified way) how fear develops. Something threatens our security — it might be a person, a disease, something that has happened, or could happen — anything at all. Different things can threaten at different times. We react by turning away from it; we try to escape. But we escape at a price, because it is in the turning away that we create fear and have fear.

The fear is not so much in the threat as *it is in our negative reaction to it.* When we come to this situation again, as we inevitably will (not least because we are afraid we will), we will feel a more urgent need to escape. In our mind we will turn away all the more quickly, and so the fear will grow and spread. We can end up being paralytic with fear.

If our experience of fear is long-standing, it might not even occur to us that things could be different; we take our problem for granted. If we know that fear brings about what we fear, that only adds to our misery. We end up being afraid of being afraid, and so our problem is compounded. Very likely no one else knows the nightmare kind of life we live. It is not easy to talk about, and in any case, who would really understand and be able to help? The Bible says, "fear has torment;" they are some of the truest words that have ever been written.

Overcoming fear

What can we do to rid ourselves of this burden? Well, the first requirement is to admit that we have a problem. That can be a hurdle to overcome in itself. People easily feel threatened by this sort of thing, and they defend themselves by denying it or passing it off. To face up to it can make them even more fearful at first than continuing to live with it. Christians often feel they have to keep "a stiff upper lip." To admit to being plagued by fears would be "to let God down." So they are unable to confess their true feelings, even to other Christians, because this would mean taking off their mask and revealing their inner selves. The truth of the matter is that we only face the problem of fear when we have to — yet we choose to.

The next thing to realise (and this is the very important point) is that as far as God is concerned, *we do not have to be afraid.* "God has not given us a spirit of fear."[5] Fear does not come from God. "There is no fear in love...he who fears is not perfected in love."[6] More than this, God also provides for us *to be made free from our fears.* "Perfect love casts out fear."[6] Instead of fear, he gives us "power and love and a sound mind."[5]

This means that we don't have to turn away in fear. Instead we can turn towards the problem and affirm the victory over fear that Jesus gives. We are to counter what will otherwise be a fear-thought by putting in its place thoughts and words which express what God provides and what he wants us to have. For example, "Thank you Father that you want me to have power and love and a sound mind. I affirm that I am now drawing on this by faith through Jesus our Lord. Praise God!"

We must continue to do this whenever we are threatened by fear. We fight the fear by *filling our mind* with strong faith affirmations of what we believe we are receiving from God. And we *continue to make those affirmations* until the fear falls away. We have already seen how three people — the man with the back injury and the two women — one with the migraine and the other with the melanoma — affirmed their healings by faith and continued to affirm them, until their difficulties fell away. The principle is exactly the same with fear. "I will not let you go, unless you bless me"[7] expresses the essence of it.

Like Carol Peterson's migraine, the fear might well come back on some other occasion. But this time, we will not only know what we should do; we will be more confident that the fear can be defeated. So again we hold on to what God wants us to have by expressing it in positive statements of faith. We defend ourselves from the fear that is trying to get in by an effective use of the shield of faith. By doing this each time the fear threatens, we will find that it comes back less frequently, and that it becomes progressively easier to repulse. Eventually we will come to the place of healing where the fear will not come back again. Faith has progressively become sight.

There might be those who would say that this is just "positive thinking" or "mind over matter." That would be a very superficial and misleading assessment of what has been presented. We have said that we are to draw on the promises of God by the sort of faith which does not doubt. If this is to be meaningful (as it has to be) it must issue in our being wholly positive, not only in our prayer, but in our subsequent thinking.

James brings this out most clearly: "Let him ask in faith, with no doubting, for he who doubts is like a wave of the sea that is driven and tossed by the wind. For that person must not suppose that a double-minded man...will receive anything from the Lord."[8]

The prayer of faith is being positive in word and thought about what God has promised and is doing through Christ and by the Holy Spirit.

If lack of forgiveness is the great *barrier* to our faith, then equally, if not more so, fear is its great *enemy*. So face your fear. Affirm the power and love and soundness of mind that God wants you to have. And keep on affirming that by faith until the fear is cast out and is no more. It is as simple as that. It is as direct as that. *And it works!*

Healing grows like a plant

So far we have been dealing with the matters that need to be cleared away if our faith is to grow. We now come to the more positive aspects and see what is meant in the last passage of scripture quoted at the beginning of the chapter.

In this scripture our Lord likens the kingdom of God to the planting of a grain of mustard seed, which grew and became a tree. On another occasion he describes the growth in a slightly different way and says, "first the blade, then the ear, then the full grain in the ear."[9] The nature of the kingdom is to grow from being minutely small to being fully developed.

Divine healing is part of the kingdom of God. That is what Jesus meant when he said, "Heal the sick and say, 'The kingdom of God has come near to you.'"[10] This means that because the character of the kingdom is to grow, the character of healing is to grow as well. Where there is faith, the essential nature of divine healing is to increase in reality until it is seen in perfection.

When we pray the prayer of faith, and our faith is equal to the mountain to be moved, whether it be for healing or for anything else, then we can expect to see the answer at once — or at least very soon. But when we think of all the barriers there can be to the effective exercising of our faith, as we discussed in Chapter 2, as well as those of unforgiveness or fear, we begin to see why the answers to our prayers usually come in a more progressive way. "According to your faith" — meaning in proportion to your faith — "be it unto you,"[11] Jesus said. So often the mountain is big and our faith is small.

When this applies we need to realise and keep in mind what we have just said — that the essential nature of the kingdom of God, which includes healing, is to grow. Our role is that of the gardener; by faith we plant the seed and then watch it come up. In particular we are to act on the only instruction given in the New Testament as to how we are to continue in prayer. In Colossians 4:2 we are told to "continue steadfastly in prayer, being watchful in it with thanksgiving." This means that we are on the watch for signs of growth..."first the blade, then the ear...," and we are thankful to God for the growth as it takes place.

Suppose we plant a seed in the ground. For a while afterwards we see nothing at all. There is no sign of what we have planted, and we might be tempted to think nothing is happening. If we could see the seed, we would realise that quite a lot is happening but none of this is apparent to us as we wait and watch. So having planted the seed and waited while nothing *seems* to be happening, we find, as time goes by, a slip of green poking its way up through the soil. We are glad — even thrilled to see it. And, as we go on watching it each day, tending it as best we can, it continues to grow and in due time reaches its full size.

And so it is when we pray the prayer of faith for healing. God says that his blessing will grow like a plant. We plant the seed by accepting healing in the same way as we accept Christ for salvation. At first we may not see any result at all. Even so we believe something is happening, and sooner or later we will see the first sign of healing appear. Our part is to be on the lookout for this improvement, however slight, and to return thanks to God. We are "being watchful in it with thanksgiving."

Exercising the faith we have is as simple, as direct, and as practical as that. You will find that you can follow through the most extensive answers to your prayers by this very simple scriptural procedure. Big doors swing on small hinges. Perhaps it will help us to understand this better if I now explain how I put this into practice with people who come to me for help in the ministry of healing.

How to continue in prayer

After I have prayed the prayer of faith for someone who wants to draw upon divine healing — that is, after I have accepted healing for him — and after I have helped that person to accept healing for himself, I arrange for him to come back and see me again. Depending on the particular circumstances, the person comes back in a week or fortnight, and then I sit him down and ask what has been happening. I encourage him to talk naturally and just to tell me about himself since we last met.

Sometimes, to begin with, the person will talk about his difficulties, and for a while the picture he paints might seem a rather gloomy one. But we have prayed the prayer of faith together — I have accepted God's blessing for him, and he has accepted God's blessing for himself. And so, I am listening to what he is saying with my "spiritual antenna" fully extended — I am listening for the slightest signal of response to that prayer. I am looking for the first sign of "the blade," if not for "the ear."

And I find (and this will be encouraging to any reader seeking divine healing himself or for others,) in almost every case where we have really accepted God's blessing by faith, that before he finishes telling me what has been happening, he has mentioned something that indicates an improvement in his condition. Already there is some answer to our prayer of faith; already the healing has begun.

When I hear of some change for the better, then I begin to sing the Hallelujah Chorus — to myself, of course. I praise God for what improvement there is, because that is all I have to do — that is all any of us has to do. Afterwards, I help the person see, from his own words, what has already taken place.

When I pray for him on this second occasion, I simply thank God for *whatever blessing has come*, however small it is. It might be only "the blade," the merest slip of green showing out against the previous circumstances of his life. I just say, "Thank you Lord for this change and improvement. It is a sign of your kingdom-healing and we return thanks for what has so far taken place. As we acknowledge what you are doing, we know you are being enabled to complete the work."

That is all I say when I pray with the person I am ministering to on this second occasion. *I do not worry about what still remains to be put right.* Whoever heard of a gardener who was dissatisfied because the tree he had planted wasn't fully grown the moment it came out of the ground? As our Lord told his disciples, the children of this world are wiser in their generation than the children of light!

I encourage the person to continue seeing and claiming his healing in this way. I get him to come and see me again, and again I just get him to talk. And again I am listening very carefully, and perhaps by this stage he too is learning to be "watchful in it with thanksgiving." So, as he refers to some further area of improvement, some greater growth of the healing-plant, something more for which we can give thanks, we praise the Lord together for what has taken place since his last visit. And so it goes on. Remember that the character of God is to complete that which he has begun. The "mustard seed...became a tree."

A real-life application

Let us look again at that true and wonderful story in Chapter 1 of the young boy who developed a spinal deformity and who was growing up to be a hunchback — one of the most distressing deformities anyone can have.

This led his parents to read the Bible with a new sense of seeking. The truths they found were those that we have been discussing in these last two chapters. They saw that God honours his promises if we pray the prayer of faith. They saw that healing is part of the kingdom of God and that the kingdom is within us. They saw that when we believe, the kingdom-healing grows, and that all we have to do is to be thankful for what growth there is.

Mark and Dorothy Bailey coined certain expressions which put these scriptural truths into more everyday language. Instead of speaking about the kingdom of God, they would say: "The perfection is within you." When they wanted to emphasise that the kingdom *is within you*, they put it like this: "Why ask for what you've got?" And when it came to explaining what is meant by the prayer of faith, they said: "You have what you accept." Strange language perhaps to begin with, but language which shows deep insight as to what the scriptural terms really mean.

Those insights became the way they lived and moved and had their being — thought by thought and breath by breath. Of course, nothing they saw in their adopted son did anything to help them. But they were not living by sight — they were living by faith. They just believed that the kingdom-plant was growing, and that divine healing was taking place in the boy. They were sure. There was nothing of "I prayed the prayer of faith, but nothing has happened" about those parents. Instead they thanked God by faith until increasingly they were able to thank him by sight. It took time, but at the end of that progressive and cumulative healing the boy was completely normal.

The scripture says: "Let steadfastness have its full effect, that you may be perfect and complete, lacking in nothing."[12] If we know what is available and how to appropriate it, there is no limit to the blessing we can draw on. And if you would like to sum up what has been said, it can all be expressed in that phrase of the Baileys: "You have what you accept."

How to increase in faith

Forgive from your heart anyone and everyone who has hurt you, so that, by God's grace, you love them as you love yourself.

Overcome fear by facing it and affirming by faith what God has provided for you through Jesus. Continue with your faith affirmations until the fear has been fully cast out.

Realise that God's kingdom blessing, which includes healing, grows like a plant from being minutely small to being fully grown. Once you have planted the seed of healing, that is, you have accepted healing by faith, all you have to do is to return thanks to God for the growth as it takes place. That will enable God to complete that which he has begun.

*   *   *

When you have thought over all these matters carefully, so that you feel you understand them, find a time of quiet to offer them to God in prayer. Pray this prayer in the most meaningful way you can. This is my prayer for you, but let it be yours as well.

Father, I confess any resentment and unforgiveness I have towards any other person at all (name the person(s) and refer to problem that has existed), and by your grace, I forgive them now, as I myself need to be forgiven both by God and by others. Lord, in as far as it is difficult to fully forgive all at once, I at least begin to forgive until I have truly done it from my heart.

I thank you that I don't have to be afraid. I now believe that by your power, your love is turning my fear out of doors. I praise you for the soundness of mind which I am drawing on and will increasingly draw on, until old things are passed away and all things have become new.

Having faced up to my problems, I now plant the healing seed of your kingdom in my life according to my need. Give me your patience as I wait for the plant of your healing to appear and while it is growing. Enable me to recognise the blade and the ear and the full corn, and to always know that it has come from you.

Lord, I thank you for the seed which is now planted and for the blessing that is now growing. Thank you because it means that you are now changing my life in spirit, mind and body; and changing the lives of those for whom I have accepted this blessing as well. My heart sings in praise that you are making us "perfect and complete, lacking in nothing." I thank you because it means that your kingdom is being extended and your name glorified.

Thank you Father. Thank you Jesus. Thank you Holy Spirit.

4

The Healing of the Memories

See to it that no one fail to obtain the grace of God; that no "root of bitterness" spring up and cause trouble, and by it the many become defiled.   Hebrews 12:15

If anyone is in Christ, he is a new creation; the old has passed away, behold, the new has come. All this is from God, who through Christ reconciled us to himself and gave us the ministry of reconciliation.

2 Corinthians 5: 17,18

WE COME NOW to an area of healing that we will look at in particular — the healing of the memories. This is a subject of special interest, partly because it is intriguing to realise that the past needs to be healed as well as the present, and also because, as we enter into an understanding of it, most of us feel that we need this healing too.

Everything that has ever happened to us during our whole life-time is indelibly recorded in our mind. In fact, our mind functions like a high-fidelity tape recorder, faithfully storing away all that we experience from the time we are born. And the recording includes not only the experiences themselves, but also the feelings, good or bad, desirable or undesirable, which accompanied those experiences. In this chapter we are going to see something of what this means in practice. We will find out more of what makes us the kind of people we are, and something at least of what we need to do, if we are to be made free from burdens that have been left from the past.

Three levels of memory

As you probably know, the mind can be divided into three parts. Firstly, there is the conscious part, which is the part of our mind we are using at this moment as we read these words and think about them. Perhaps it would be more accurate to say it is the part containing the thoughts of which we are conscious at this or at any one moment. Then there is the second part which we call the subconscious mind. This is our memory bank; it contains all the things we can remember. Some of us, we say, have a good memory; others have a bad memory. We might have a good memory for some things and a bad memory for others. But whatever our memories are like — good or bad — all the things we can recall are in that part of our mind called the subconscious.

Yet these two parts, the conscious and subconscious, even when taken together, form only the smaller portion of our mind. They are only like the tip of the iceberg that is showing above the water. The third part, the part of the iceberg that is submerged, is by far the largest. This is called the unconscious mind. And in our unconscious mind are *all* the experiences which we have had in the course of our whole life, but which we can no longer remember. They are things that have really happened to us, but which we have forgotten. And we have forgotten them so completely that we cannot bring them to mind, however much we might want to and however hard we might try.

It takes only a little thought to realise that if the unconscious portion of our mind is like the part of the iceberg beneath the sea and is so much bigger than the rest, then it must contain a great deal more of what makes us the people we are. Compared with our conscious and subconscious mind, it is the more significant part. And again, like the iceberg beneath the water, we do not see it, and we may not be aware of it; but it is there.

By using certain techniques, such as hypno-therapy, a person can be enabled to recall experiences which are stored in the unconscious mind. This is how we know that these experiences are still there. For example, under hypno-therapy you could remember what presents you received for, shall we say, your fourth birthday. You would be able to recall who you sat next to in third class at primary school, and who sat behind you and in front of you. It is all there, just as though a vast tape-recording machine was running continuously in your head. Each experience you have had — whether for good or for ill — is on the tape and is still there. And if you were able to play that tape-recording back, every detail would come out just as it happened at the time.

All these experiences which we have had, whether they be in our mind at the moment, or are able to be recalled, or are now deeply forgotten, have left their mark on us. Some of these experiences have been good and happy and productive, and they have brought us joy and peace and strength. But others have been less fortunate, and some have been trauma- tic. They were the times in our lives when there was fear and resentment or some other negative happening, and they have been hurtful and damaging to us. Very often those difficult experiences might not have been our fault. Perhaps we were the victims — innocent victims — of circumstances. But that doesn't alter the fact that, whatever the experience was, however it came about, and whether it is remembered or unremembered, it is there to stay.

Here, of course, we are describing what has happened to us in a rather black and white kind of way. In practice, it is much more complicated than this. Our experiences are strung out like washing on the line; they go through the whole range of reaction, from very bad to very good, and everything in between. Neither can any one experience be thought of in isolation from others. In practice, one experience, whether it be good or bad, will tend to "trigger-off" the same reaction in similar circumstances later on. In this way the strength or the weakness becomes more deeply ingrained. It has a cumulative effect; confidence begets confidence, and fear begets fear. The end result is that we are highly complicated personalities, the sum balance of all that we have inherited and acquired.

Although we need to guard against over-simplification, we don't want to go to the other extreme by thinking it is all so complicated that we cannot do anything about it. If you have to wash an elephant, you have to begin somewhere!

The general point I am wanting to make is that, just as past experiences that have been good continue to have a good effect on us in the present, so past experiences that have been bad exert a bad effect on us now. This is why parents should be concerned about the experiences and associations their children have in their formative years. They need to realise that what is happening to their children now is not only important as far as the present is concerned, but will largely determine the kind of men and women they are going to be for the rest of their lives. This is only too true, as I have come to realise over the years I have been involved in the healing ministry.

Let us look carefully at some illustrations from real life which will demonstrate what I am wanting to share with you in this chapter. As you think about them, I hope you will feel they are speaking to you too, because we are each the product of our experiences, and in varying degrees we all need this kind of healing — the healing of the memories.

Expelled at six

John and Amy Stephenson were referred to me because they were having acute trouble with their six-year-old son, Jeremy. He had been expelled from school. And if someone who is six has been expelled from school, you can be sure that you have a real problem on your hands! Jeremy had so misbehaved in class, screaming and fighting, that he was regarded as uncontrollable. In the interests of the other children he was finally asked to leave, and he was referred to the school psychiatric service. There was some delay in drawing on this resource because of a change in staff, so in the meantime the parents came to me.

His mother said he was as "nice as pie" when his father was around, but when he was on his own with her he would turn into a very objectionable little boy. He would look at his mother with hate in his eyes, and his tantrums were getting more and more out of hand. The more his mother gave into his demands the more demanding he became. Yet the more difficult he was with the mother, the more agreeable he was with the father. It was so bad that it had been suggested that he was possessed and needed deliverance!

After I had heard the parents' story, I asked, "Has he always been like this, and if not, when did it first begin?"

"It began when he was two," Mrs Stephenson explained. "Before that everything was normal, and after that it began to go wrong and has been getting worse all the time."

So I asked the obvious question, "What happened when he was two that could explain the change in him that has taken place?"

The story went like this: Jeremy was a much wanted and loved baby. As the youngest in the family, he tended to be spoilt by his parents and older brothers and sisters. At first there were no problems, but when he was two his parents took into their home two other children who were in need of foster parents. Mrs Stephenson in particular tried to make up for what the two new children had lacked in motherly love, so her attention was now divided between them all. At first Jeremy was fretful, then he started to misbehave and it grew worse and worse. They hoped it might get better when he went to school, but when he was separated from his mother in this way he became uncontrollable.

The explanation for his asocial behaviour was simple. He

had been over-accepted to begin with, which meant that, when two other children were suddenly introduced into the bosom of the family and obviously took some of mother's attentions, Jeremy's nose was put well and truly out of joint. His fretfulness was a sign of this, but it had not been understood and constructively reacted to. The tantrums were a further way of drawing attention to himself and trying to get back the attention that he had always been used to. This was addressed to the mother because, as a child, he was specially dependent on her, and because it was the mother who had been concerned to give love to the two new children. It was a copy-book illustration of present problems being caused by past events.

I explained this to John and Amy, and said that the way forward was to believe that God was healing these past hurts. And not least, Jeremy needed to be healed of the over-love he had received to begin with. I helped them to react to the tantrums in a positive way, so that they affirmed by faith that God was healing the events that were causing the disturbed behaviour.

The parents did their best to follow this through, and they called me on the telephone when the going was tough so that I would add my faith to theirs. I was interested in what Amy said to me later. "I have proved to my own satisfaction that when I react negatively to Jeremy's tantrums and become tensed up, he only becomes worse. But when I react in positive faith, he quickly changes for the better and becomes a nice little boy again."

It took some weeks, but not too long. Once faith for healing began to be exercised, Jeremy quickly improved until the nightmare became a thing of the past. He is now a normal little fellow; he has restarted in a new school and is doing well; and his mother and father know how to handle every situation with the prayer of faith.

When a child misbehaves consistently, there is more than an even chance that he is really saying, "I'm feeling hurt, would someone please help me?" And what he needs usually is the healing of hurt memories.

Reaching back seventy years

Every year the Cathedral Healing Ministry Congregation have a conference at the magnificent Anglican Conference Centre, "Gilbulla", which is some 70 km. from Sydney. One of our activities is a prayer laboratory — a time which is set aside for people who want to learn to pray more effectively. I referred to this in a previous chapter and explained how we went about it. One of the members on this particular occasion was a woman in her seventies named Hilda Johnson. When I invited people to come forward for this exercise in believing prayer, Mrs Johnson said, "Canon, will you pray for the healing of the memories for me and for my sister as well?"

I said to her, "Would you like to tell us something of what you want us to pray about? Then we will be able to pray more intelligently and effectively."

"Well," Hilda replied, "this is my story. When I was a little girl there were only three of us — my mother, my sister and myself. And our mother preferred me over my sister. I was always the favoured one. My sister felt left out; she felt lonely; and she felt resentful. She couldn't 'take it out' on our mother, because she wanted mother's affection. So she 'took it out' on me. There was constant quarrelling and none of the happy relationship which girls growing up should have shared. But it isn't just that. Time has made the difficulties worse. And here we are now, in the last years of our lives, still without the closeness that we should have. Would you pray that our memories be healed — both hers and mine?"

So we laid hands on her and I prayed for her myself. In brief it was something like this: "Our loving Father, we thank you that one of your great and precious promises is that those who are joined to Christ are made so completely new that old things have passed away. By faith, we believe that we are drawing on that blessing for Hilda who all her life has been lonely, and also for her sister who all her life has been resentful. We believe that you are now healing their memories by your love and power. Thank you that you are enabling them to enter into the *full* reality of being new creations in Christ. We praise you for this by faith, and through Christ our Lord. Amen."

After the conference had ended, Hilda went back to her home in Queensland. She had no opportunity to be in touch with her sister, who lived 900 km. away in a country town. But during the following week, she telephoned me in excitement to say: "Canon Glennon, my sister has invited me to go and stay with her for a holiday. She sounded so friendly! I'm going next week."

So off she went, and there followed a most natural, and continuing, reconciliation between the two of them. When Hilda came back from her holiday, she wrote to me: "I never told my sister about our prayer, but, do you know, we were sisters for the first time in our lives. And we really loved each other."

Do you see now how we can be in bondage to the events of the past? It could be a lifetime ago. In this case it was seventy years. This simple and beautiful story is all the more valuable because it finds an echo in many a heart. Not that the circumstances would be identical, or even similar to those of Hilda Johnson, but the principle of the story could have a poignant relevance to many. We all need the healing of past experiences that have us in bondage, and will have us in bondage for ever, unless we can be set free. And the only person who can really do this is God, for his wonderful provision is that the old passes away and the new comes.

Grasping a nettle

Once again the story is centred at "Gilbulla", where we were having our annual conference. We were about to commence a meeting when two members of the congregation,

Steven and Elsa Davis, arrived to see me. They make a practice of giving hospitality to people in need, and on this occasion they had with them a young woman who was staying in their home.

This attractive young woman, Sue, had been involved in a car accident. Before it happened, she had been a happy, healthy, normal young adult. She had not been injured physically in the accident, but as a result of it she had suffered a total amnesia, a complete forgetfulness of all that had happened. She could not remember one thing about it, but instead of returning to a normal life, she had gradually become what can only be described as a mental vegetable. She had been to psychiatrists who had done their best for her, but there had been no improvement in her condition. So Steven and Elsa brought her to our meeting and asked that we have special prayer for whatever was causing this trouble. I knew nothing more of the problem than this.

As it happened, there was some reason why I needed to pray for her straight away — I think Steven had only a little time available. So I excused myself from the group I was leading and asked my colleague, the Reverend Len Harris, to take over, explaining to them what I was going to do. I have a reason for saying this, because when I went out of the room to pray for the girl, Len immediately called on everyone to pray for her too. And I am sure it was their group prayer, with its corporate faith that was the means of bringing about what then took place. With Steven and the two women I went to the library, where we could be quiet and undisturbed.

Sue could offer no help as to what was troubling her so deeply, because of her total amnesia. So I stood behind her, placed my hands on her head and began to pray, letting the Holy Spirit lead me. After I had been praying quietly in this way for some fifteen minutes, trying, as it were, to let God take over, to my great surprise I "saw" the accident! In my mind's eye it was night time, and I saw two cars. I knew that Sue was the driver of the car on the left, and I could see the other car slewed across in front of it, but a little distance away. There was someone, a man, in the driver's seat of this second car. And as I looked at him, I realised to my horror that he was dead. I did not know it in any other way, but during this time of deep prayer the Spirit of God revealed to me these details of the accident.

Sometimes when I am driving my own car, I think how terrible it would be if I had it on my conscience that I had been responsible for the death of another person in a car accident. This helped me to realise that, because this young women knew she had killed this man, she could not forgive herself. She could not face up to what she had done. She could not carry on with her life. And this was why she had a total amnesia. This was why she needed to forget everything that had happened. She simply could not face the awful reality of it.

I now began, gently but plainly, to refer as I prayed, to what I now knew. "Lord, I see there was an accident," I prayed, "and I see that it was a serious accident..." (come to the point slowly — don't barge in — you can easily make more problems than you solve.) "I see that it had far-reaching consequences, and I can see that someone was injured, and injured so badly that he died...Lord, this is why Sue cannot face herself. This is why she cannot forgive herself... As a result of this accident...she has killed a man."

As I continued to spell out the trouble in this way, carefully, plainly, and with a reliance on God, and taking much more time than I am indicating here, she began to groan within herself. It was not so much with her lips — it seemed rather to come from somewhere deep within her. And then at last, having spelt out what all the trouble was, without leaving out any detail as she saw it, I began to pray that God would heal her of this memory. Because, you know, when we have done all that we can do, we have to leave behind the things that are past. We have to go on living. God has other things for us to do. If our lives are to be of any further use in the present, we simply cannot go on living in the past.

And so I believed that God was healing her memories — healing all that this traumatic experience had been to her, by the prayer of faith and the prayer of love. I continued to pray and to believe for the healing of her memory, until there wasn't one more word or one more thought that needed to be expressed. This is when we come to the end of this kind of prayer. And now, after nearly three-quarters of an hour with her, I had finally reached that point. All the people in the next room had been praying for her also, adding their faith to mine. Now I knew there simply wasn't another word, or another ounce of faith that I could share with her. It was finished! And so I thanked God in the name of Jesus.

Sue was no different when we had finished. But I knew that the prayer of faith had been prayed and I praised God for her healing by faith. Then Steven and Elsa took her home. And from that time on, progressively and quickly, she completely recovered. She could remember everything that had happened, and she could face it. She began to live again, for that is what God wanted her to do.

Of course others had known that Sue had been involved in this fatal accident. Even so, they had not been able to use this information so as to effect any change in her. But I did not know about it at the time. Rather, the Holy Spirit revealed that fact to me through the gift of knowledge, and the prayer of faith enabled it to be used for the healing of her memories.

Perhaps the pastoral point might be made that when one is trying to help people who have done what they believe is wrong, no attempt should be made to "butter them up." One should not try to minimise the problem by telling them they couldn't help it. That won't assist in the least. The problem has to be looked at the way they look at it. In this case, I had to see it the way Sue saw it and begin there.

And when a nettle has to be grasped in a counselling situation, it needs to be grasped very carefully and firmly and with a dependence on God. It is easy to make things worse; it takes more skill to make things better.

Outside faith for forgiveness

I would now like to discuss a third aspect of the healing of the memories. It illustrates something else that is important to many people. Once again the circumstances will differ from person to person, but the principle remains pertinent to many a situation. This particular story concerns a sincere and active Christian I know who told me this story herself. The details are confidential, so it must be sufficient for me to say that Mrs Kay had done something that was wrong. But though she had been fully forgiven by others concerned, she could not forgive herself or even believe that God had forgiven her.

Many people have this problem, especially if their guilt is associated with something for which they have a great sense of remorse. It is difficult for anyone to have a full assurance of forgiveness in these circumstances. They bitterly accuse themselves and blame themselves over and over again for the great wrong they have done and the harm that has been done to other people — a harm which they feel will affect their relationship with them for all time. They can even feel they have become castaways from God.

And so it was in the case of Mrs Kay. Things got worse and worse because of this great burden of conscience, and she finally reached the point where she was unable to carry on. Then she went to a psychiatrist. Fortunately for her, the psychiatrist she consulted was also a Christian, and when Mrs Kay had told the story of her felt guilt, the psychiatrist said to her, "You don't need psychiatry, you need God's forgiveness."

She said, "Of course I believe in God's forgiveness, but I just don't experience it; I have such a great feeling of guilt."

"Well," replied the psychiatrist, "our Lord said to his disciples, 'If you forgive the sins of any, then they are forgiven.'"[1]

"In my particular church we rather steer clear of that sort of thing," — said Mrs Kay, unconvinced.

"It's in the Bible," the psychiatrist argued. "If you're repentant, and if you're believing in Christ for forgiveness, then I can add my faith to yours that you are forgiven. That's what it means, don't you see?"

And so the doctor said to his burdened patient, "We're going to kneel down." And they knelt down on the floor of the psychiatrist's surgery and he then prayed a prayer something like this: "Lord, we thank you that one of your provisions is that if we confess our sins, you are faithful and just to forgive our sins and to cleanse us from all unrighteousness. This, your servant, has done wrong and she has confessed it. She is believing in you for forgiveness and I now add my faith to hers that she *is* forgiven and that she *is* cleansed. And by the authority committed to me as a Christian, I remit her sins and I say that they *are* now forgiven, through Christ our Lord. Amen."

The woman told me that from that moment, as though she was a pilgrim kneeling at the Cross of Christ, the burden of her guilt completely rolled away. And it never came back. From that time she was free, because she *knew* she was forgiven. And she was able to make a new life for herself.

Whatever our problem is, we need the appropriate healing ministry from God. And so very often, the healing that we need most is the forgiveness and cleansing of *past* events. It is our responsibility to claim these things by our own repentance and our own faith in Christ. If we have the assurance of forgiveness and cleansing because of the faith we are exercising, then praise God! But if, because of our feelings of guilt, we find it difficult, or even impossible, to enter into the reality of that forgiveness and cleansing, then it is time for us to go to some trusted Christian friend, or to a Christian minister or priest, and ask them to add their faith to ours — for that is what confession and absolution means. They are outside our particular situation and their faith is comparatively objective. Outside faith needs to be added to inside faith; that is what is needed, and that is how it works.

The emotional causes of physical illness

So far we have looked at the healing of a hurt in a child and the healing of an experience seventy years old. We have seen an example in which there was a revelation of what needed to be healed, together with the healing of that extremely traumatic experience itself. And we have looked at a need for forgiveness and cleansing where "outside" faith needed to be added to "inside" faith. As a final point, we are now going to consider one further aspect of the healing of the memories which is both interesting and very important.

Griffith Evans was a Doctor of Medicine and a Fellow of the Royal College of Surgeons. Before he died a few years ago, Griffith Evans published the results of some of his clinical studies. He maintained that in people who tend to be sensitive (and I suppose that description applies to most of us to a greater or lesser degree,) a series of difficult experiences could have a cumulative effect until the point is reached where one more problem becomes "the straw that breaks the camel's back." It could be anything causing resentment, anxiety, sorrow or any other heartfelt problem. The important point is that the final problem has ongoing significance. It isn't something they get over. It is a nagging and continuing burden. Dr Evans went on to maintain that within two years, the emotional burden could issue in physical illness. The sick mind leads to a sick body.

Medical men vary in their opinions as to what percentage of physical illnesses have their origins in emotional factors. At a teaching mission I was once leading in St John's Cathedral, Brisbane, I quoted one medical opinion which affirmed that 60 to 70 percent of physical problems are emotionally caused. The presenting problem is a physical one, but it has been brought about by emotional factors in the person's life. Afterwards, I was approached by one of Brisbane's leading specialists, who was also an active Christian. He said to me, "With respect to you, Canon Glennon, I don't agree with the figure you quote. In my opinion it is 90 percent!"

I follow Griffith Evans' insights in my own ministry. If I explain how I go about it, that will help to make my point and give the balance I seek to have. If someone comes to me with a physical illness, I ask him how long he has had the trouble. He may say, "Six months ago in May this year."

I will then say to him, "I want you to think back to more or less two years before that, to May two years ago. Did something happen then, or since then, which was important to you and which had continuing significance?"

You would be amazed at how many people will immediately answer this question by relating some truly traumatic experience that has been of lasting significance in their lives. The same can apply to children. The following are two examples of cases I have encountered that illustrate what I am saying.

A mother's burden

Joyce Griffin was a regular member of the Healing Ministry Congregation, and she came to me saying that she had a lump in her side. She had made an appointment to see a surgeon, but as he was on holiday, it was going to be a fortnight before she could see him. She asked if I would pray with her for divine healing. As well as talking about faith for her physical healing, we talked together along the lines we have have been discussing here. It was not new to Joyce, but sometimes it is a help to talk about things person to person.

I asked her, "Did something happen about two years ago before this problem showed itself?"

"Well, Canon, that was about the time my son was divorced, and now he's remarried. I'm a Christian and I just can't reconcile myself to what has happened. I keep thinking about it and I feel hurt deep down."

"Well Joyce," I said, "I can see it from your point of view. But it is no good reacting to it so that you make a problem for yourself. That could be your trouble."

"I know, but what can I do?"

"Well, the Bible says that we are to cast our burden on the Lord and that means that we don't carry it around ourselves."

"I've tried to do that," she replied, "but I take it back again. Before long I'm worrying again."

"I understand," I replied, "but I'll tell you what we can do. Let us pray about it together and I will believe it for you. We will believe it together. That will help a lot." And so we did.

You know, when we see what is wrong, and we have to do something about it, it is amazing what faith we can have. We have to, yet we choose to. I met with her every few days and worked the matter through, both in counselling and in prayer. We prayed about both the physical problem and the background emotional difficulties.

After she had been coming for the fortnight before she was to see the doctor, Joyce was able to say that the difficulty she felt about her son's divorce had been completely overcome. She was no longer burdened by it; the burden had been cast on the Lord and it was left there. Then she went to the surgeon and he examined her. He couldn't find the lump, so he asked her to stand up and show him where it was. She couldn't find it either. The lump had gone! And there has been no recurrence of it.

"The root of bitterness"

As well as the two-year period we are talking about, this illustration concerns what the Bible calls "the root of bitterness." Bob Barrington told me of a deep and continued disagreement he had with a work colleague. Bob had shown a generous attitude towards this other man in their business relationship only to find that he was taken advantage of, so that the man continually harassed him in order to take more advantage. Bob felt hurt by this, and a resentment built up towards his colleague. I knew about it and used to tell him that the devil of resentment was that it was justified. He saw the point, but was unable to extricate himself from the situation. So the resentment continued.

Some two years after this resentment had come to a head, Bob began to notice a large area of roughness and discolouration on his neck. The skin specialist was noticeably disturbed by its extent and diagnosed it as "multiple hyperkeratoses" or skin cancer. This is not cancer in the usual definition of the disease. It is a pre-cancerous condition which can be effectively treated but can leave unsightly scars.

There was an unavoidable delay in proceeding with medical treatment, which gave Bob time to reflect on the matter of his resentment towards his colleague at work. In a way that he could not explain, yet was meaningful to him, he became convinced that there was a link between his resentment and his skin condition. Up to that time he had not done anything about the resentment, but now he felt he had no alternative but to face up to it and do something positive.

Meanwhile, the business associate had moved interstate, and though there was not the personal contact, the relationship was still a bad one. Bob therefore wrote to him addressing him for the first time by his first name, saying that he regretted the trouble between them and asking for forgiveness for his faults in the matter. It was the first time he had expressed any kind of regret; until then all he had ever done was to blame the other man. After all, wasn't he right?

A reply came back also expressing regret for the misunderstanding, with the writer admitting for the first time his own failure and guilt in what had happened. The most unhappy episode was over. Bob knew that he could now forgive and forget. The skin cancer shortly disappeared without medical intervention and did not recur.

I am not suggesting that the presenting problem always clears up automatically once the underlying causative factors have been dealt with. As far as my experience goes, this case of Bob's skin cancer is the exception rather than the rule. Usually both areas need to be recognised and dealt with in an effective way. The main point of the case histories examined here is to show something of the varying circumstances in which there can be a period between the emotional problem and the physical consequence.

The point should be made that what Griffith Evans says is an hypothesis: a possible explanation for which he produces clinical evidence. No one is being dogmatic. But it is an hypothesis brought forward by an eminent medical practitioner and it seems to fit the circumstances of many people. In as far as it is valid, or something like it is valid, it becomes vital for the understanding and treatment of illness as well as for the understanding and practice of prayer for healing.

Perhaps it ought to be put in more general terms. It seems to be agreed that the majority of physical illnesses are emotionally caused. This means that if the people who have that kind of illness are going to be healed and made whole, the emotional causative factors have to be healed as well. The first requirement is to know what these emotional factors are. What will come to light here will depend on the hypothesis used and the questions that are asked. Then something has to be done that will remove their effect. Otherwise, only the end result is being treated while the cause remains untouched.

People need to be made whole. Spirit, mind and body need to be healed; and the past as well as the present. God says to us, "If anyone is in Christ, he is a new creation; the old has passed away, behold, the new has come." Our point has been that so often it is "the old" of our lives that needs healing if that wholeness is to be there. The old memories...sorrows ...experiences of yesterday and yesteryear — healed so that they have "passed away" and healed so that "the new has come."

Do you need the healing of the memories?

Give it some quiet but very careful thought. If you can't do that right now, set aside a time when you can. Not only as it concerns you, but you may well think of others who have this need. Face the problem and bring it into focus in your mind. Often we don't want to face something in our past which has been hurtful, but face it we must if the memory of it is to be healed. So face it squarely and bring it clearly to mind so that God can deal with it.

This book is intended not only to be a discussion of the principles of divine healing — it is to help you pray the prayer of faith for healing. When you are ready, pray this prayer very thoughtfully, and feel that I am praying it with you — that my faith is being added to your faith.

Father, I stand before you as one of your children. I know that you know me as an individual and that you love me perfectly. Before you, all hearts are open and all desires are known, and no secrets are hidden from you. I now open my memories to you so that you can come in and help me. I have carried these burdens for so long. You know the hurt, sorrow, resentment and fear that have been my companions. Sometimes I think I have never been happy — anyway, not as others are happy. I have tried to get along and do the usual things, but inside I am alone and afraid. I am sorry for myself, but I feel I have some reason to be sad. I now surrender it all to you.

From this time onwards, I am going to believe that you are changing me and making me the kind of person you want me to be. I affirm that you are now coming into my whole life with your wonderful love, with your ointment of healing and your new life.

You say in your word that the things which are loosed on earth are loosed in heaven. Thank you that you are now loosing from me all the negative experiences of my past, remembered and unremembered. You say in your word that if we are joined to Christ we are made into new people. Thank you that the old things are now passing away and that all things are being made new.

I praise you for giving me this new start. I am beginning to believe that I am a brand new person inside. Thank you, Father, that Jesus is giving me his life so that I have a new life. I am walking with you. By faith I believe you are making me whole. Keep me close. Amen.

5

The Power of the Holy Spirit

You shall receive power when the Holy Spirit has come upon you.

Acts 1:8

Brother Saul, the Lord Jesus who appeared to you on the road by which you came, has sent me that you may regain your sight and be filled with the Holy Spirit.

Acts 9:17

Did you receive the Holy Spirit when you believed?

Acts 19:2

Be filled with the Spirit.

Ephesians 5:18

IF THE THINGS we have been considering in the previous chapters are to become practical realities in our lives, it is essential that we draw on the power of the Holy Spirit. For the Holy Spirit is that person of the Trinity who is in the world, and who brings to life what the Father has provided for us through Christ. Without this power, the provisions of God and the prayer of faith remain academic and dry, things which we know to be right in theory but have great difficulty putting into practice. For this reason we need to understand the resources of the Holy Spirit; he is the key to our being changed from being power-less to power-full.

Power to witness

While we certainly need this power to make divine healing a reality in our lives, it is equally true that we need this same power of the Holy Spirit in every area of our Christian activity. Healing is but part of the ministry which our Lord committed to us as members of his church. It may be helpful, therefore, if we first examine this need for power in relation to another major area of ministry in which we are or should be already involved.

When our Lord told his disciples that they would receive power when the Holy Spirit had come upon them, he expressly stated that the purpose of this power was to enable them to be witnesses for him. So, we need to ask ourselves, do we have the power that enables us to tell others about the Lord? The real question is, do we do it? When did we last talk to someone about Jesus? Because that is what a witness is — one who tells what he knows and has experienced.

If we are doing this and, as a result, men and women are being made new in Christ and are becoming part of his church, then it can be said that we have the power of the Holy Spirit. At least we have it in that particular area of ministry, and there is no reason for us to do more than we have already done in drawing on this blessing. That of course does not leave out the need to increase in power and become more effective witnesses as we go on in our Christian life. But as far as we have gone, we have good reason to believe that our Christian witness is as it ought to be — we have drawn on God's power and it is working out in practice.

But, and this is a very big "but," if we are *not* telling others about Christ so that they are being joined to him, then quite clearly we do *not* have the power of the Holy Spirit as God means us to have it. We may have a very sincere and meaningful experience of Jesus ourselves; we may worship regularly in church; we may pray and read the scriptures and go frequently to Holy Communion. All this is good. But if we are not witnessing, then we need to take stock of ourselves to make sure that we are not merely taking refuge in these other things, because our Lord has made it perfectly clear that he requires us, and that the Holy Spirit enables us, to confess him to those he places across our path.

If we lack this power that our Lord wants us to have in his service, we have to admit our need and take appropriate action. St Paul tells us what we are to do. To the Christians of his own day he said, "Be filled with the Spirit."[1] He would say the same to Christians today.

Much has been written in recent years about the power of the Holy Spirit and no doubt much more will be written in the future. As we have only this one chapter in which to consider its application to the healing ministry, we will confine our examination to our need to "be filled with the Spirit." So let us first look at some illustrations from the scriptures and from contemporary life and then go on to receive some instruction that will enable us to draw on this blessing for ourselves.

Are we filled with the Spirit at conversion?

Some may well be asking at this point, "Are we filled with the Spirit when we are converted?" The answer is that we need to see the difference between being "*born* of the Spirit"[2] and being "*filled* with the Spirit."

When we are converted and believe on Christ for salvation, we begin a new life. Our Lord used the analogy of birth to show what is meant here — "You must be born anew."[3] It is a beginning, it is our initiation into Christianity by which we become alive to God. And it is a work of the Holy Spirit — we are "born of the *Spirit*." When we speak about being "*filled* with the Spirit," however, we mean receiving the power for the ongoing Christian life. Paul said that we need "to be strengthened with might through his Spirit in the inner man."[4] This is the only way we can be kept close to God and be used in his service. In that context and for that reason, Paul said, "Be filled with the Spirit."

There seems no reason why a person should not receive the fullness of the Spirit, so that he has power for service, at the time of his conversion. What happens at that point in his life will depend on his vision of what is available and the faith that is exercised by him and for him. But it also has to be said that in the early church, the fullness of the Spirit was regarded as something separate and subsequent to Christian initiation. With some people the interval between these experiences was short; with others it was longer. But there *was* an interval.

We can be thankful that the church today has, on the whole, a clear concept of the need for conversion by which we become the children of God. At the same time we need to realise that, by and large, it has lost its awareness of the need for Christians to receive the Holy Spirit as power for service. I believe this is why the church, generally speaking, is so impotent in its witness and ministry. For it is trying to do all the work of God on that experience of the Holy Spirit which is intended only for our initiation as Christians — meaningful as that is.

Like the early church which Paul visited at Ephesus, we hardly know that there *is* a Holy Spirit — at least not in the sense that he is a person as much as Christ is a person, with a range of ministries that come from him alone. Instead, to most of us, he is a being who is often mentioned in formal worship, but whom, in reality, we disregard because he (or very likely "it") is someone whom we do not know in a personal way. The next step, in effect, is to rationalise him away.

That is why it has become acceptable with many Christians to say that the gifts of the Holy Spirit are not for today. What those brethren fail to grasp is that when we are filled with the Spirit as a second blessing, our life and ministry is transformed in a way that we had no awareness of before we drew on that blessing. We then find to our astonishment that we don't have to explain anything away; the Holy Spirit and his ministries are all wonderfully true and real!

The testimony of Scripture
    After Paul (or Saul as he was then known) was converted

on the road to Damascus and called Jesus "Lord," he was
taken to the city where he waited three days before Ananias
came to him at the Lord's direction. "Brother Saul," declared
Ananias, laying his hands upon him, "regain your sight and
be filled with the Holy Spirit."[5] From this we can see that in
Paul's case, conversion took place first (for no one can call
Jesus "Lord," but by the Holy Spirit), and then he was filled
with the Holy Spirit three days later.

There are some who say that this only means that his
conversion was spread over three days. Even if that is so, what
we are saying still applies: i.e. if conversion ending up with
being filled with the Spirit can be spread over three days, it
can be spread over any time at all. But there are good reasons
for affirming that what happened on the Damascus road was
Paul's real conversion and that what happened three days
later was a second and subsequent experience.

The reasons are:

1.   In response to his enquiry, "Who are you, Lord?" the
Lord said, "I am Jesus of Nazareth whom you are persecuting." Then Paul said, "What will I do Lord?"[6] In calling
Jesus of Nazareth "Lord," he was now doing the very same
thing for which he had been persecuting others. Later in 1
Corinthians 12:3 he said that no one can say "Jesus is Lord"
except by the Holy Spirit. Thus, it is evident that Saul of
Tarsus acknowledged Jesus as Lord on the Damascus road
through the Holy Spirit. He was trusting him, believing in
him, and committing himself to Jesus for salvation.

2.   Three days later the Lord quietened the anxieties of
Ananias that he was being sent to the erstwhile persecutor of
the Christians by saying, "Go, for he is a chosen instrument of
mine to carry my name before the Gentiles..."[7] Here we have
evidence that God acknowledged Saul of Tarsus as a servant
and a believer and a chosen vessel. This was the divine
witness to Saul's conversion.

3.   When Ananias came to Saul, his first words were an
acknowledgement that Saul now belonged to the Christian

community, for he addressed him as "Brother Saul..."[8] The Greek word, of which Brother is a translation, means "out of the womb, brother or relative."

4. Ananias expressly said that the purpose of his ministry, as given him by the Lord Jesus, was that Saul regain his sight "and be filled with the Holy Spirit." This done, other matters were then attended to. There had been no previous opportunity for him to be baptised. Throughout the three days following his conversion he had been blind, fasting and in isolation. Now he arose, was baptised, broke his fast and had fellowship with the disciples at Damascus.

Here then we have a threefold witness to the fact that Paul was converted on the Damascus road so that he believed in the Lord Jesus Christ through the ministry of the Holy Spirit. Complementing this, we have the clear statement that three days later he was filled with the Spirit.

If there can be an interval of three days between being converted and being filled with the Spirit, then there can be an interval of three years, or any time at all in a person's life. Once we have established the principle that these experiences do not have to occur simultaneously, then it makes no difference how long is the period between.

Similarly when Paul, now converted and filled with the Holy Spirit, went to visit the church in Ephesus, one of the first questions he asked was, "Did you receive the Holy Spirit when you believed?"[9] At that time he knew nothing about these people except that he assumed they were Christians. With that in mind he asked his question. But their answer showed that he had taken too much for granted; they had not even heard of the Holy Spirit, and their belief in Christ was very imperfect.

Paul proceeded to correct this, and when they fully believed on Christ he baptised them as a sign of that. After this he laid his hands on them that they might receive the Holy Spirit. And they did. These were separate acts and separate experiences, however closely the one followed the other. So whether we look at the matter in the light of Paul's first question, or in the light of what happened afterwards, it is clear that Paul saw the receiving of the Holy Spirit in fullness as something that could happen, and in fact did happen, subsequent to conversion.

The same thing happened in the case of the Samaritans referred to in Acts, chapter 8. Philip had come from Jerusalem and proclaimed Christ to them, and as a result of what they heard and saw Philip do, they turned from their old way of life to the new life in Jesus. They repented, they believed on Christ for salvation, they were born again. And because of their belief they were baptised in water. In other words, the Samaritans received their Christian initiation.

When the apostles in Jerusalem heard that the Samaritans had accepted Christ but "had only been baptised,"[10] they sent Peter and John to lay hands on them that they might receive the Holy Spirit as well. To believe on Christ for salvation and be baptised is wonderful beyond our full understanding — it makes us members of Christ, children of God and inheritors of the kingdom of heaven. Yet here it was said that the Samaritans "had only been baptised." And so concerned were the apostles for these new converts to receive *all* that God had for them, that two of their number made a special journey to Samaria to pray for them.

The work of Christian initiation in the Samaritans had certainly been the work of the Spirit. They were born of water and of the Spirit, just as we are when we become Christians today. But it is quite obvious that what the apostles understood by "receiving the Spirit"[11] was something different from and additional to what had already happened.

The events we have been considering vary in detail. That is only to be expected, because different events bring out different aspects of all that is involved. For the same reason, experiences of conversion also differ between individuals. But there is one detail that remains solidly consistent in these scriptural accounts: receiving the Spirit in fullness occurred *after* conversion.

It is unfortunately common in the church today for many to regard these and similar instances in the New Testament as unique events with no relevance for present-day Christians. But that is to make an assumption for which there is no scriptural authority whatever. It says, in effect, that God has recorded the unique and not-to-be-repeated things, and has left us ignorant of what is normal and what applies to our situation. Yet Paul tells us that "all scripture is profitable for teaching."[12] That can only mean that these narratives are teaching in action and teaching for us.

Present day testimony

Let us now proceed from scriptural examples to some present-day testimony which can do much to show that God intends *us* to share in this same provision. First, an illustration of what the fullness of the Holy Spirit can do for a whole country:

In Latin America, where there is a nation-wide emphasis on the need to be "filled with the Spirit," there is as a result one of the dramatic success stories of modern missions. Despite the great social changes that are taking place in that continent today, despite the far-reaching political and economic upheavals that have been occurring for years, a large proportion of the Christian churches in South America clearly know what they are about; they are going from strength to strength, and there is tremendous verve and vitality in their ministries. So much so that, though there were only about 50,000 Protestant Christians in Latin America at the beginning of the century, their number had reached 1,000,000 by the 1930's and it has passed the 20,000,000 mark in this decade! This annual growth rate of 10 percent is three times that of the country's general population increase — yet the Latin American population growth is one of the highest in the world. At this rate of increase it is estimated that by the year 2,000 the number of Protestant Christians in South America will reach 100,000,000!

Recently published accounts of this emphasis on witnessing and winning people to Christ and other manifestations of the Spirit in the South American churches read like a 29th chapter of the Acts of the Apostles! When I asked an Anglican clergyman (one *not* involved in the charismatic renewal) who had recently returned from a visit to South America, why it is that these churches are witnessing so effectively and bringing such great numbers of people into a living relationship with our Lord, he replied, "It is because of their experience of the Holy Spirit."

My own experience

I should now like to add my personal testimony of this experience and to refer to some turning points in my own life and ministry. I hesitate to make personal references, but at least I know them first hand!

I became a Christian when I was a late teenager. After that I could truly say, in the words of the old hymn, "Nothing in my hand I bring, simply to thy cross I cling." On the strength of that commitment I went through theological college and was ordained into the ministry of the Anglican church. I have always been a loyal and happy member of my church, and as the years went by I was basically content. That is, with the exception of two nagging doubts.

One was that I did not increase in my experience of the things of God from one year to another. It was rather a case of "as it was in the beginning, is now and ever shall be!" My other doubt was over the fact that I did not see much result for my ministry. There was a great deal of organisation and activity, but people did not seem to be committing their lives to Christ as a result. There was some blessing, but not much. One of the things that some of my brother clergy would say was, "God doesn't require *successful* ministries, he requires *faithful* ministries." That was all right as far as it went, of course, but it seemed to me to be something of a rationalisation.

Then I became involved in the healing ministry. This very soon brought home to me, as nothing else had, the need for more of God's power in my life than I had ever drawn on before. And I suddenly realised what a "successful" ministry you can have through mere organisation. If you can put words together, you can pass as a good preacher. If your parish has various active groups within it so that all ages are provided for, you can have a family-like church life. If you employ a reputable fund-raising organisation, you can have an assured income. In fact, I have come to the conclusion that if God the Holy Spirit was withdrawn from the church, 80 percent of our activity would continue on unhindered!

Organisation has its rightful place, but when you are face to face with the need for someone to be healed, preaching a good sermon makes not the slightest difference, a well-organised parish is utterly beside the point, and dollars and cents have no value whatever. It is then that you realise your need of the power of the living God and that nothing else will do!

Six months after I became involved in this ministry, Agnes Sanford, that great and gentle teacher of the healing power of God in the world today, was visiting Australia and came to conduct a teaching mission at St Andrew's Cathedral in Sydney. During that time I came to realise even more how much I needed the power of the Holy Spirit in my life if my own healing ministry was to become really effective. When I told Mrs Sanford this, she said, "Do you know that if you have not yet been filled with the Holy Spirit, you can be filled now?"

"No, I didn't know that," I answered, "I thought it all happened at conversion and that there was never any more."

"You *could* have received that fullness when you were first converted if you were believing for it, and if so that is good," she explained; "but if you did not receive it then, you can receive it now."

I shall not go into detail about her ministry to me, except

to say that Agnes prayed deeply for me on three occasions. The end result was that I felt I was being *immersed* in the Holy Spirit. It was as though something like a dye had gone all the way through my being, in contrast to a stain or colouring that was previously only skin deep. I certainly knew that something wonderful had happened to me.

It was an experience of the same order as my conversion. Just as my conversion many years previously had been a watershed in my life so that I was radically and permanently changed, so too was my experience of being filled with the Spirit. There was the same contrast between what it was like before and afterwards, and also the same permanence. My conversion had made me *alive* unto Christ; now being filled with the Spirit enabled me to *witness* about Christ. I had always *tried* to witness, but now the Holy Spirit gave me the *power* to make it an effective reality.

Some Christians, I know, find it difficult to accept that there is more that God wants us to have after we are converted. But usually these same brethren have no difficulty in believing that God wants to have more of *us*. I see no difficulty in approaching the matter in this way if it helps them to go further in their Christian experience. When we remember that our bodies are the temples of the Holy Spirit, it is perfectly reasonable for us to pray that our bodies be given over to the full possession of the Holy Spirit. Surely that is what is meant by the expression "be filled with the Spirit." Having said this, however, it has also to be said in truth and love that those who approach the matter in this way, seldom testify to a vital change that has taken place in their lives as a result.

What happened as a result

Following this wonderful experience I was quite different, and so was my ministry. For the first time, ten years after my ordination, people began coming and asking me to minister to them. I would just tell them about Jesus and find that they would respond to him easily and naturally. I simply told them what he meant to me, and they became believers by the exercise of their own faith. I remember one man, Alex Miles-Smith, who came in the first place for healing, describe it as "the time Jesus called me to his side."

I found, too, that I could lay hands on people and pray that they be healed and they were healed; if not immediately, then in a progressive way. I found that I could believe for people to be filled with the Spirit, as I had been, and they would draw on this new dimension of spiritual life. The things that I was already involved in, like the sacraments of Baptism and Holy Communion, the rite of Confirmation, and worship generally, all came to life in a new and remarkable way. In a special way I was made alive to the person and ministries of the Holy Spirit — something of which I had been unaware and unaccepting beforehand.

My prayer life also became very different. For a long time before I was filled with the Spirit, I did not seem to be able to pray in a meaningful way. It wasn't that I did not pray. It was just that the problems in my life and ministry had built up because I didn't have the spiritual resource to meet them. As a result my prayer life had become dry and shallow. Becoming involved in the healing ministry helped to a degree, but it also gave me a much bigger barrow to push!

No one knew of this problem, and I tried to make it appear as though nothing was wrong. But after I had been filled with the Spirit, I found I could not pray enough! I would get up early in the morning so that I could have more than an hour just for prayer. Perhaps this is the most satisfying thing that happened — and continues to happen. For nineteen years have now gone by and my joy in praying continues. I think I would rather pray than do anything else!

I also found, rather to my surprise, that the Bible became a new book to me. In the course of my ministry I had read the Bible continually and I thought I knew what was in it, especially the New Testament. But now it took on a new reality. I found that when the Holy Spirit shows truth to be truth, it is as though you had never known it before. Up to this point in my life I had known many of these truths in my mind — now God enabled me to know them in a new and living way.

And this unfolding has continued. Instead of my life and ministry always seeming the same and never progressing to anything better or more effective, I began to find that God was ever breaking fresh truth to me, so that I had a growing relationship with him. I can only say that it has been like going on a pilgrimage. For the first time in my Christian life I do not consider that I have arrived, but am "straining forward to what lies ahead."[13]

I do not want to give the impression that being filled with the Spirit does away with all your problems or that you cannot fall into sin again. On the contrary, I have many more problems than I ever had before! For it is not only the Holy Spirit who is active in a new and living way; so too are the devil and his ministering spirits! "He prowls around like a roaring lion;"[14] Peter warns in his epistle. Life never seems to be easy and sometimes it is very hurtful. At these times God is saying, "You have further to go in trusting me and being made like me." In fact, a person who is filled with the Spirit sometimes feels that God has got him by the scruff of the neck and that there is always a mountain ahead to be climbed!

The reason that I have referred to myself at some length is because basically I am a very ordinary person, and I want to encourage all others who think of themselves as ordinary Christians to go on and be filled with the Spirit so that they too can be better servants of Christ in the world. For all who draw on this power say, as in my own case, that it impels them to talk about Christ. For the Spirit does not speak of himself, but reveals Christ to us and to others.

Sometimes when a testimony like this is given, it is explained away by others who say that what is being talked about is conversion. This is quite untrue as far as I am concerned, for I was truly and soundly converted in earlier years. As I now see it, that was my initiation into Christ. What subsequently happened gave me power for service so that my ministry as a Christian could bear fruit. Others say that it is "psychological," whatever that might mean. But how can spiritual fruit be born from something that is only subjective or psychological?

Could it not be that the right explanation is the one given by those who have drawn on this further dimension? At least they have the advantage of seeking to explain what they have experienced, whereas those who have not experienced it, not unnaturally, seek to explain it away. Despite other differences, those who have had this experience unite in testifying that they have been "filled with the Spirit."

What are the requirements?

At this point we might well be asking where we need to be in our Christian walk if we are going to receive the Spirit for service, and what attitudes of mind and heart are necessary? Two things need to be said.

In the first place we must be committed to Christ. No one can receive the Holy Spirit for on-going service unless he has first believed on Jesus Christ for salvation. This was noted earlier in the chapter. Paul was first converted so that he called Jesus "Lord," and after that he was filled with the Spirit. Later he was concerned that the people at Ephesus had a proper acceptance of Christ before they received the Spirit. And with the Samaritans, there was first belief on Christ and baptism in water before the apostles laid hands on them that they might receive the Spirit. This also is my own testimony.

If you already believe on Christ you are ready to proceed. If not, you need first to come to the Saviour in repentance, faith and obedience. If you are converted but unsure whether you have been filled with the Spirit, then the effectiveness or otherwise of your Christian life and ministry will clearly provide the answer. Are you fighting a paper-war, or are souls being added to the Lord? You will have no doubt about your real position if you will allow God to lay the truth upon your heart.

The second requirement is that we set no conditions or limitations on *how* God will fill us with his Spirit. Too often people say, "Oh, I want to be filled with the Spirit, but I have a hang-up about speaking in tongues," or "I'd like to be filled with the Holy Spirit for this particular purpose." What they say might be sincere, but it amounts to laying down guidelines for God to follow, or specifying to him what function the Holy Spirit is to serve in their lives. In effect, the Holy Spirit is being asked to fit in with the person's own pre-conceived ideas!

It makes no difference what these ideas might be — we cannot ask God to fit into our viewpoint. Whenever we come to God, whether to be converted or to be filled with the Spirit, we can only come in unconditional surrender. We come like children, ready to let him have his way entirely, ready to receive all that he has for us.

Frequently I find good, well-intentioned Christian people disillusioned and disappointed because they do not seem to be able to receive the fullness of the Spirit they so much desire. On further enquiry, I find that they still have some problem or hang-up about it. There is nothing wrong with that; indeed, we need to encourage people to bring out their questions or doubts or reservations and to try and help them so that their problems can be overcome.

But the fact remains that we have to resolve our reservations *before* we can receive this blessing from God. Why? Simply because while we are still wrestling with our difficulties, we are quite unable to come to God in that state of surrender which allows him to do just what he wants with us, and which allows him to give us all that he wants us to have.

How to be filled with the Spirit

Having taken careful account of what is necessary for this blessing to be ours, and having dealt to some extent with the misunderstandings that so often surround it, we are now ready to consider the vital matter of *how* we receive the Holy Spirit in his fullness. Basically it could not be more simple, because, as with all God's promises, we receive the Holy Spirit simply by praying the prayer of faith.

In Chapter 2 we looked in some detail at a particular example of the prayer of faith that is widely understood and effectively practised. The instance was that of Christian conversion. We saw that if a person is to be converted, he has to come to the point where he accepts Christ as Saviour and Lord. And though he may be changed in a moment, we saw that in most cases people do not experience anything straight away. So we tell such a person not to rely on his feelings, but on his faith. We tell him that he must exercise faith, and this means believing that Christ *has* come into his life, though he *feels* no different. The more definite the person is that he has accepted Christ and acts upon this in faith, the more easily will that person enter into the reality of having Christ in his life *in point of fact*.

That is the principle of the prayer of faith. We follow through that principle as we pray the prayer of faith for healing; and the way we pray to be filled with the Holy Spirit is the same again. Whatever the promise of God that we desire to draw upon, the prayer of faith by which we appropriate it is followed through in exactly the same way. "Whatever you ask in prayer, believe that you have received it, and it will be yours."

This simply means that you ask for and accept the fullness of the Spirit so that you then believe you have it. You make a decision which you can look back on as something that you know you have done. From that time on, you affirm by faith that you are so filled. If you have difficulty in having faith for yourself, then ask others to add their faith to yours so that there is corporate faith. This is how it was done in the early church, which means it is how we can do it too.

What happens in fact will be in direct proportion to the reality of the faith that is exercised. If you deeply believe to the point where you do not doubt, you will be changed in a moment. But if you are not blessed in this way immediately, there is no need to be discouraged. We have seen that where our faith needs to grow, God graciously makes provision for our prayer to be answered progressively. We have seen this to be so in conversion. It is certainly so in healing. It is often so in the matter of being filled with the Spirit. But as you continue to affirm what you have accepted and believe you have received, acting it out in practice, then sooner or later you will come into the full-bodied experience of this blessing with "signs and wonders"[15] following.

The important thing is to have faith — and not to be over-concerned about the signs. So often, I find that people seeking this blessing are badly advised to concentrate on the *signs* when they should be concentrating on *faith*. Faith is the part of the transaction that is our responsibility; the signs are God's part and are his responsibility. If we are concerned to do our part properly, there will be no lack on God's part. Yet so often people get it round the wrong way and try to do what only God can do, while failing to do what only they can do—Jesus says to us still, "only believe."[16]

The laying on of hands

At this point some may be wondering what part the laying on of hands plays in receiving the fullness of the Holy Spirit. In the illustrations we have studied from the early church, the laying on of hands was used each time people prayed for others to receive the Spirit. But it is also clear from scripture that there were other times when the laying on of hands was not used. The initial outpouring of the Holy Spirit on the church on the Day of Pentecost is a case in point, as is the "falling" of the Spirit on those who had gathered to hear Peter in the house of Cornelius.

How essential, then, is the laying on of hands for the receiving of this blessing? The answer is that it is appropriate and can be very helpful — but it is not essential. It is helpful because it has a sacramental meaning; it is the outward and visible sign of the inward and invisible faith which one person shares with another when he prays for him. It is not essential because, as we have seen, the blessing can be received without it. Let me illustrate this latter point.

I was speaking one night at a parish hall in Sydney on how to be filled with the Holy Spirit. I explained that the laying on of hands was helpful and desirable, but not essential. In the congregation was a university student, and though he did not ask for ministry at the conclusion of the meeting, he did buy a book on the subject from the book-stall. He chose "Nine o'clock in the Morning" by Dennis Bennett of the Episcopal Church in the United States.

A day or two later this student, while waiting to attend a lecture, was sitting in his car at the university, reading his book. As he read he became convicted of his need to be filled with the Holy Spirit. All his former reservations melted away and he wanted to exercise faith for this blessing. Remembering what he had heard at the meeting he said to himself, "Why shouldn't I be filled with the Holy Spirit right here and now?" So in his heart he prayed, "Lord, I ask for and accept this blessing as a gift. By faith Lord, I affirm I am now filled with the Holy Spirit." And immediately he was conscious of being filled with the Spirit and was overwhelmed by the love and power of God.

Final instructions

I now address myself particularly to those of you who, perhaps for the first time, have been brought to realise that there is a further dimension of spiritual power available, and that you need this fullness in your own life. The point I have just made is that you can appropriate this blessing for yourself — you don't have to go off looking for someone to pray for you, and you don't have to wait for some other opportunity to present itself. Rather you can pray for and accept the fullness of the Spirit for yourself, right where you are, simply by believing for it.

If you want to do this, first be quite sure that you know what you are about to do, and that it is something that you want with your whole heart. You should only act on it when all your reservations have been dealt with, so that you come to God in complete surrender and dependence on him. When you are ready, I suggest that you pray along the lines of the meditation that follows. I am believing that all who use it will be richly blessed by God, so in a real way it is also my prayer for you.

Loving Father, I thank you that you have brought me to know Jesus and for all this has meant to me. I return thanks for what the Holy Spirit has done in enabling me to be a channel of your blessing to others. I confess I have so often failed you and I ask your forgiveness for every shortcoming.

I come to you now because, despite what blessing there has been, I am deeply aware that there is so little fruit from my ministry that I can offer you. So often I have been like the talent that was hidden in the ground. Father, I need to be filled with your Spirit so that I have power for your service. It is the desire of my heart and I come to you with no reservation. Do with me as you will.

I now ask for and accept the fullness of the Holy Spirit as a gift from you, and by faith I thank you that I now have it. I believe, Father, that my body, which is the temple of the Holy Spirit, is now being immersed in that Spirit. I believe that my mind is now being transformed so that I have the mind of Christ. I believe that my whole being; body, mind and spirit, is now given over to the perfect infilling of the Spirit of Christ.

Father, I thank you for the blessing I now have by faith, and I will praise you until I have it by sight. But whether it be by faith or by sight, I praise you that I am now filled with the Holy Spirit to the glory of the Lord Jesus Christ and the extension of your eternal kingdom. Amen.

To those of you who have already drawn on the fullness of the Holy Spirit as well as to those who have just accepted this blessing, I would say: keep on being filled with the Spirit. We all need to have faith for its continuing reality in our lives. And if you would like a final word of guidance, remember that faith means praise. So praise God — and keep on praising him!

6

Stretch out Your Hand to Heal

1. Praying *with* other people

As thou didst send me into the world, so I have sent them into the world.   John 17:18

You are the body of Christ and individually members of it.
                                                          1 Corinthians 12:27

THE STATEMENT IN Christ's prayer that we are sent into the world by him in the same way as he was sent into the world by the Father, lays a great responsibility on all Christians. It is our responsibility both to do what Christ has said, and to do it in such a way that will enable the kingdom to be extended in the lives of those to whom we are sent. If we are to be effective, we must act in a way that is in itself grounded in the scriptures.

In this connection St Paul makes it clear that there is to be a balance between discharging our individual responsibility and working as a team. Both are needful. We have not so far placed any real emphasis on the corporate side of the ministry of healing, but now, in the first part of this chapter we will remedy that omission.

The church of Christ
Let us bring to mind something of what God has revealed

to us about "the church." The church is nothing more or less than the people who believe in Christ for salvation and who seek to live this out in their lives. It is the fellowship of all believers, irrespective of denomination and the kind of place they meet in. True it is that there are denominations and church buildings, but they are secondary. The church is the body of Christ, part of which is on earth, with the larger part in heaven.

St Paul explains something of what the church is like by using the striking simile of the human body and its various parts:[1] one part is an arm, another an ear, another the nose, an eye, a tooth, etc. Each part of the body performs its own distinctive function, which makes it both indispensable and yet wholly dependent on every other part. Every part needs to function perfectly, but that function can only be meaningful when all the other parts are functioning and the body is acting as a whole. It goes without saying that no part of the body can live to itself — it is each for all, and all for each.

So too with the church and its members. Every one has a unique ministry which complements all the other ministries. The important dimension is the *whole* ministry of the church, though that is only the sum total of all the members. There is true and full interdependence in the body of Christ. St Paul expresses it all so clearly when he says, "You are the body of Christ and individually members of it."

The healing ministry of the church

The encouragement given in this book to the individual to stretch out his hands to heal should be thoroughly understood in this wider setting. Every believer has a part to play in the healing ministry, but he does that in relationship to the part every other believer is playing as well. It will be what the *church as a whole* is doing about the healing ministry that will be the measure of the final outcome.

The individual will be strengthened by this, but he will

also be limited. He will minister to and with others, and in turn will receive ministry from them; but these things in themselves mean that he will not just be "doing his own thing." Let us look at this in the area of the gifts of healing and the ministry of the elders.

One of the ways in which the ministry of divine healing operates is through a gift of healing. Paul speaks in 1 Corinthians 12 of these various charismata or gift ministries, including that of healing, and says that they are given by the Holy Spirit "to each one individually as he wills."[2] You may know of someone who has a gift of healing, or you may have one yourself. God has given such people a special endowment of spiritual power, by which they are able, in Christ's name, to lay hands on others to heal.

It is interesting that in the list of spiritual gifts, healing is the only one that is described in the plural. All the others are expressed in the singular. We do not know why this is so, but the most likely explanation is that there can be different gifts of healing for the various kinds of physical and mental disorders. Roland Brown, of the Camp Farthest Out organisation, says that if a person who has asthma comes to him for healing, he straightway begins to praise God, because he has a gift of healing for asthmatics. And if I myself have any gift of healing, it is to do with fear. Because I understand that type of problem, I am able to relate to those who are sick with fear and to pray for them effectively.

At first sight these illustrations may give the impression of the individual going his own way. But that isn't what is happening at all. As we have already seen, it is only as each and every Christian shares his or her gift ministry, that we have *all* the ministry God provides for the church. We can see from this how completely interdependent we all need to be, yet how important is the part each one of us has to play.

We will see these principles further brought out if we turn again to what James says, "...call the elders of the church..."[3]

In these circumstances the elders of the church are to be the channels of healing for the person who has called them; yet there is no suggestion that they have a gift of healing. True, they will have a gift ministry of some kind, and with one or more it may be that of healing. But that would be incidental. The particular qualification they have in this situation is that they are the representatives of the church. And because they represent the body of Christ, God administers divine healing through them. Here again are individual Christians, in this case elders, fulfilling their ministry, but in the context of the church fellowship and on its behalf.

What we are saying here can be looked at in another way. We are realising more and more that it is not only the clergy who represent the church. Certainly, by reason of their ordination, the clergy have a special role of leadership, but other believers are equally much the church because we are all equally joined to Christ. It follows that each member will equally represent the church, though the form of representation will vary.

It also has to be said that *all* Christians have, or are intended to have, ministries that are, more or less, equally effective. In the infant church, we see things happening as God really intended them. Even the humblest Christians, e.g. the deacon Philip, had a ministry equal to that of the apostles in its effect. The same principle still applies. We will have ministries that vary one from another, but the same reality of Holy Spirit blessing should follow each and every one. These things make us all the more a team in which everyone plays his or her part.

A note of warning

What has been said will be underlined if we see what can happen when these guidelines are not observed. When first we began to extend the ministry of healing at St Andrew's Cathedral in 1960, many people came to realise, for the first time in their lives, what great power God had given them as members of the body of Christ. And some of them, though well-intentioned, were misguided enough to go around laying hands on people in their own wisdom, and quite outside the discipline and guidance of the rest of the church. In this sense they acted irresponsibly, and I am afraid I have to say that sometimes they created more problems than they solved.

So I sincerely trust that no one reading this book will take it upon himself to act in any way that is less than responsible, or unmindful of the awesome trust that God gives us as believers. For this reason I would urge you to extend this ministry within your local congregation, under the guidance of and in co-operation with your priest or minister or elders — and not to do anything in the name of the church without consulting them or having their approval.

The Order of St Luke

Another very desirable step to take, if you really want to further the healing ministry of the church, is to become a member of the Order of St Luke. This Order, which is world-wide as well as inter-denominational, seeks to restore the ministry of healing to its rightful place in the church. No one may belong to it unless he is first a member in good standing of his local denominational church. By joining this Order, you will also gain inspiration and guidance from other members, both clergy and laity. And you will find that your own ministry will have a much greater acceptance, as well as being infinitely more effective, than if you just tried to minister on your own.

As Christians, God calls us first to respond to him individually, but then, having done this, to act together as a team, as members of his body and members of one another. There is no such thing in the New Testament as the Christian who "goes it alone."

Receiving ministry

A further point needs to be made. Just as we need to pray

with others to *extend* ministry, so we need to pray with others to *receive* ministry. Experience has shown that those who "go it alone" in praying for their own need of healing often end up in difficulty.

Faith for yourself can be a very subjective experience. When you have the pain and anxiety, it can be virtually impossible to "believe that you have received" healing so that you "do not doubt in your heart." And because faith is then not lived out as it has to be, healing does not come. Disillusionment and depression can follow, so that the last stage is worse than the first.

This is where we need the outside and comparatively objective faith of others to be added to our own faith. It can be hard enough for the outsider to have faith that does not doubt, but where many make what contribution of faith they can, the corporate faith can be very effective indeed. We all need the understanding and support of other Christians who will commit themselves to ministering to our needs, not just on an isolated occasion, but in an on-going pastoral way. When this happens, experience again shows that no problems result from this ministry, but rather the sick person draws on a rich and ongoing blessing of God that builds him up in his real-life situation.

We are to "call the elders of the church." This implies that we are members of the church, that we involve the church in our need situation, and that the church responds in a way that is meaningful. I earnestly advise those who would draw on divine healing to do so in a truly corporate way. It is the only safe way.

A prayer

Loving Father, I thank you that you have made me a unique person and that you care for me as an individual. I thank you too that you do not want me to be alone and that in various ways you have made me a member of a family. I rejoice in the earthly family I belong to; for the wider family of friends, and especially for my family in Christ.

I confess that I have not always thought about these things in the ways that I should, and because of that, my life, and the lives of others, has been the poorer. I have often taken what I know for granted, even though I have experienced the blessings and insights that have been referred to many times.

I now give myself sincerely to a new realisation of what my place in the body of Christ really means. I pray the prayer of faith that I enter into its ever-increasing reality, its creative discipline and its perfect blessing. Thank you that when I don't have my own way, it is because you want me to have your way. Thank you for every circumstance you permit so that I will be brought to faith in prayer and be made complete, lacking nothing; for myself, for others, and for the extension of your kingdom.

Lord, this is my continuing prayer.

Amen.

2.   Praying *for* other people

They came, bringing to him a paralytic carried by four men... And when Jesus saw their faith, he said to the paralytic, "My son, your sins are forgiven... I say to you, rise, take up your pallet and go home."

Mark 2: 3,5,11

We have so far been thinking of *the need to pray with* other people. We now turn our attention to *how to pray for* other people.

We do not need to discuss the basic dynamic of faith in prayer, because that has already been done in previous chapters . We now want to apply this to the matter of *praying for people other than ourselves*. It is what might be called *vicarious* prayer. And just as we need to be crystal clear in our understanding and practice of prayer for ourselves, so too we need to be thoughtful and detailed in our prayer for others, if our ministry is to be effective.

Prayer for someone else's healing

Let me explain what I have to say with an illustration. Bill and Barbara Smith-Hughes came to see me because Bill was a chronic asthmatic. They were both Christians, but as far as healing was concerned, the wife had faith but the husband was full of reservations. Bill was a solicitor and wanted to explain his point of view to me. I was quite ready to listen to his "submissions," but I could see that I would be in for a long session! So I said to him, "I am quite happy to have a conversation with you, but would it be acceptable to you if today we do not concern ourselves with *your* faith, but that you let *me* have faith *for you*? You have had faith to come, and your wife has a meaningful faith, let me believe on your behalf."

He replied, "No problems — please carry on."

So I prayed along these lines: "Father, your servant has a need and you have made a promise to raise him up. I now pray the prayer of faith on his behalf. I believe that he is now receiving healing for his asthmatic condition. I accept healing for him and I thank you that because of my faith, healing is now flowing to him and will continue to flow until he is perfectly recovered, through Jesus Christ our Lord."

Whenever I thought of Bill after that I disciplined my mind to say, "Thank you Father, you are healing our brother now." When he came to see me a week later he was noticeably better. I prayed with him again, as Jesus prayed again for the man at Beth-saida, and on two other occasions after that, by which time he was completely healed. He has had no further attacks of asthma.

"I haven't one reservation left," he told me later. "I want you to know that I have come to the point where I simply and fully believe in healing, and I believe in healing for myself."

His faith in healing has never faltered since that time. More than that, he is active in sharing his faith with others.

Prayer for someone else's conversion

Another illustration will emphasise what we mean by vicarious faith; this time of how we can pray for a need other than healing.

I was once approached by a man and his wife, John and Marie Forster, whom I knew and greatly respected. They were both devoted Christians and active in church work. Marie opened the conversation and said, "We're very worried about our daughter Ruth. We have no reason to believe that she is a Christian. She never darkens the church door. Could you help us?"

Their daughter was a young married woman, and though parents and daughter had a good relationship in many ways, they felt they could not approach her on this matter. "Because if you raise something with her that she doesn't like, she just puts up the shutters," John explained. So they asked me to pray about it, and I said I would. I should explain that I did not see the daughter following this request, which meant there was no kind of personal ministry with her. It all had to be done by prayer — vicarious prayer.

I prayed like this: "Loving Father, I praise you that it is your desire that everyone 'be saved and come to the knowledge of the truth'⁴". We therefore know that it is your will that Ruth be joined to Christ in salvation. Thank you that her parents have had faith to ask me to pray as well. I now pray the prayer of faith for her salvation. I believe that the Holy Spirit is so ministering to her that she is being enabled to respond and put her own faith in Christ as Saviour and Lord. I praise you that you are bringing this about now so that your kingdom is being extended. Amen."

I did this so completely that from that time on, I only

thought of Ruth as being converted through the Holy Spirit's ministry. I was so committed to this that I did not doubt in my heart.

Some eighteen months later, I met her parents again, and this reminded us of our earlier conversation. "Do you remember how we asked you to pray for Ruth?" Marie asked. I was able to reply that I certainly remembered and that I had been praying for her.

"Well," her father came in, "we ought to tell you what happened. Ruth has joined the church! She is the leader of the girls' work in the parish, and her Rector has told us what a wonderful influence for Christ she is with everyone with whom she comes into contact!"

What had happened was that my faith (and the faith of her parents) enabled Ruth to come to faith herself. Our faith was not a substitute for her faith, but it enabled the Holy Spirit to minister to her so that she accepted Christ by her own act of belief.

Let me develop the point further with one more illustration: Not long ago, I conducted a parish mission at Sandgate in the Diocese of Brisbane. I had been speaking on this same subject and afterwards a woman approached me. "There is something I would like you to know," she said. "My minister heard you say this on a cassette. As a result, he believed that his son would be converted and he came to Christ. When I heard this," the woman continued, "I said to myself, 'If that is good enough for my minister, it is good enough for me. I am going to believe for my husband's conversion.' And so I did. Now he is not only converted, but has been filled with the Holy Spirit, and is in theological college studying for the ministry!"

As you can imagine, that made my day!

Vicarious faith in infant baptism

There is nothing new in the principle of vicarious faith. In the Anglican church we apply this every time we have infant baptism. As a result of the baptism, the Book of Common Prayer affirms "that this child is regenerate and grafted into the body of Christ's church."[5]

But why are we able to make this profound statement? After all, we are saying that the baby is now a Christian! We are able to say it because the parents and god-parents have had faith for and on behalf of the child. Their Christian faith has so availed *for* the child that it is just as though the child has faith himself. Faith for the child is so completely shared by others that it is counted to be faith in him, even to the point where we affirm that he is now a Christian.

At least that is *one side of the coin.* The other side is that the faith being acted out for the child (and which of course must *continue* to be acted out) enables him *to come to faith himself.* Liturgically this is expressed in the service of Confirmation. Here the young adult says in effect, "Once the Christian faith and life were affirmed on my behalf in my baptism; now I am confirming this by my own faith, and will continue to do so."

If only parents and god-parents and clergy fully realised what they are doing in infant baptism and believed for the child in a complete way, it would issue in results entirely different from what is now so often the case. Instead of looking at the child or young adult and wringing our hands and saying, "Oh dear me, he doesn't believe," we should look at ourselves and realise he is like that because we have not believed *for* him. And if we did, even now, he would come to faith in Christ because, in the first instance, we had faith on his behalf.

I am a god-father many times over. And I am able to say, to the praise of God, that *all* my god-children grow up to be Christians. This is because when they were baptised I prayed the prayer of faith for their conversion and believed it in an on-going way so that I did not doubt. And in every one of them this has issued in their own personal faith in Christ!

You would no doubt like to see an instance of this in the

scriptures. One of the quotations at the beginning of this section is such an example. Jesus, seeing the faith of the four men who brought the one who was sick, said to the sick man, "Your sins are forgiven," and then, "rise, take up your pallet, and go home." Others were believing for him, and Christ used their faith so that it was just as though he believed himself — for both sin and sickness.

Isn't that what praying for other people means — having faith for them? If you are still in any doubt, may I ask you this question: if *that isn't* what praying for other people means, then *what does* praying for other people mean?

I should mention at this point that having faith for others is all the easier when they already have some faith for themselves. The more faith they have, the easier it is to help them; the less faith, the more difficult. But irrespective of the degree of faith they have, praying for other people simply means we are sharing our faith with them. If they already have faith, our "outside" faith is added to their "inside" faith; if they do not have faith, then we have to accept full faith-responsibility for them. It is our faith availing *for* others and theirs *for* us, that gives prayer so much of its purpose and joy.

In this ministry for others, the dynamic of faith applies in the same way as we saw in earlier chapters. We have to know what God promises, we have to accept the blessing and to affirm it by faith, and then we are to be "watchful in it with thanksgiving."[6] Having faith for other people is exactly the same in principle as having faith for ourselves, except that we are doing it *for* them, and (most desirably) *with* them.

Sacrificial prayer

We now need to consider some of the difficulties we can encounter in having faith for other people. You will recall the instance in the gospels where Jesus' disciples had prayed for an epileptic boy but he was not healed — at least, not until Jesus came on the scene and prayed for the boy himself.[7]

The disciples had been praying the prayer of faith for healing with many other people, and their ministry up to this time had been effective. So, quite naturally, they were mystified when on this occasion they prayed for a boy and healing did not result. And they became more confused when the boy's father took him to Jesus, explained what had happened, and the boy was healed as soon as Jesus prayed for him!

The disciples' confusion was very understandable. So they said to Jesus, "Lord, why couldn't we do it?" And Jesus replied in effect, "It is because you haven't enough faith. Your prayer of faith hasn't sufficient reality. But you can take some consolation from the fact that the problem you were praying for is a bigger one than you have met before. This kind is healed only by sacrificial prayer."

None of us would want to make that sort of statement ourselves. In fact, even when we remember that this was what Jesus said, we still hesitate to relate this teaching to real-life situations today. So it might be helpful if I now give such an illustration of healing through prayer and fasting, after prayer in the ordinary way had proved ineffective.

Before I do this however, I want to reiterate yet again, that Jesus in no sense blamed the boy or his father for their lack of faith when the boy was not healed. Having said that however, we have to add that Jesus told the father, "All things are possible to him who believes."[8] Jesus made it clear that the deficiency in faith was on the part of those disciples who were praying. For this reason, it is quite wrong for us to say to a person who is sick, "You haven't enough faith." Nor have we any right to make such a statement to members of that person's family.

Assuming a person has enough faith to ask for the prayers of others, then if anyone is to be blamed for a lack of faith, it is those who minister to the sick person; the elders, or more generally the church. In fact the real reason why we don't see many miracles today, is that the church generally, the body of believers as a whole, does not have enough faith. So often the church today does not *expect* prayer to be answered in the way our Lord described in Mark chapter 11 verses 20-25, whether it be for healing or anything else. This is why it is so important for us to really understand what faith means; and that the final responsibility for it being acted upon lies with the church as a whole.

Prayer and fasting for depression

My illustration in this instance concerns a young man sick with depression who had been coming to me for ministry. He was in fact the worst depressive I have ever known — and I have met many! This young man had been coming to me at regular intervals for no less than two years. I had counselled him and prayed with him many times, and I had done everything I knew to help him appropriate healing for his condition. But at the end of two years he was just the same as he had always been.

At this stage, two members of the Healing Ministry Congregation of St Andrew's Cathedral came to me with a suggestion. "Do you think that we should fast as well as pray for Harry?" they asked. "And could we gather together a group to pray for him, rather than you doing it alone?" Immediately I accepted their insight and desire to assist in the matter, rebuking myself for not having thought of it before. It showed me afresh how interdependent we should all be as the body of Christ. And it made me see again the reality of the ministry that God gives to the laity of the church. Indeed, some lay people have a greater capacity for ministry in certain areas than the clergy.

So I said to them, "Of course. Would you please gather together some other concerned people who understand the situation, and we will arrange to meet and pray with Harry if he is agreeable." I then contacted Harry and explained what we would like to do. It is necessary to have the co-operation and understanding of the person concerned if he is going to be personally involved. Harry was agreeable to what we proposed, and we arranged to meet in one of the people's homes for this purpose.

For twenty-four hours before we came together, we all fasted. That is to say, we went without solid food. The point about fasting is that one uses the experience of doing without food to be a constant reminder to depend on God more. *In this way one thing becomes something else.* The great thing that God wants us to do, is not to trust in ourselves, but in him. And as we use our circumstances, whatever they are, to enable us to move closer to God, we are then depending more on *God*, and depending less on *ourselves*. There is, as a result, a greater release of the power of the Holy Spirit.

It is most important for us to realise that this is the meaning and purpose of fasting, and that, if we go about it in this spirit, we will soon lose the distress and discomfort of going without food. But if, on the other hand, we say to ourselves, "Oh yes, I am fasting, but I wish I wasn't so hungry," it shows that we don't understand that we should react to the hunger pangs in a positive way so that we are depending on God *more*. We only succeed in putting ourselves out of step with what we are seeking to do. And it would have been better if we had not started to fast in the first place.

On this occasion, the six of us who had agreed to minister to Harry first of all fasted for twenty-four hours, then we came together as we had planned. There we prayed the prayer of faith for him. We turned to God, we took hold of his promise of healing, and we accepted it. We all prayed vicariously on his behalf, adding our faith to what faith he had — which wasn't much because he was so sick. So we praised God by faith for Harry with as much meaningfulness and as much dependence on God as we were able. And when we had finished praying, Harry was not one whit different from what he had always been.

What were we to do now? My brothers and sisters in the ministry soon provided the answer. "We'll do it again," they said. So a week later, we fasted again, using this time of fasting to depend on God even more, and again we met together to pray the prayer of faith over Harry. We faced the fact that we had prayed for him before without having our prayers answered, by simply adding acceptance of blessing to acceptance of blessing, faith to faith, praise to praise. So again we did this until we had done everything with all the meaning of which we were collectively capable. And finally we came to the end and said "Amen!" And never in my whole life have I seen anyone so transformed in a moment of time as was Harry at that instant! He was healed and he has remained healed ever since!

Notice in this case the development in the ministry and the factors involved in reaching the end result of healing. First I personally prayed with Harry over a period of two years with all the commitment I could share with him. Then the ministry was widened to include others (a most important point) and this was accompanied by sacrificial prayer that enabled a greater release of the Holy Spirit. In spite of initial disappointment, this was continued so that faith was added to faith until he was restored to health. This experience also shows how faith is both quantitative and cumulative.

Prayer for healing is never shallow-water fishing. It requires sacrificial prayer, prayer and fasting until we are brought to the end of our self-dependence. And when we are drawing on God's direct promises, it must be done with the inward resolution, "I will not let you go unless you bless me."[9]

I remember the Principal of a Baptist Theological College saying to me after I had addressed his students: "I will tell you, Canon Glennon, why there isn't a healing ministry in every church. It is because the sacrifice required is too great!"

The blessing of Jesus

The final point that I wish to make in this part of the book is perhaps the most important one of all. It is this:

If I were asked to state the main reason why I am involved

in the healing ministry of the church today, I would say straight away that it is not simply because of healing. Though divine healing is so close to the heart of God, as we know from Jesus, and though it is so wonderful when a person is raised up in the way Harry was — his whole life changed and completely different ever since — I would have to say that, for me, healing is not an end in itself.

No, the main reason for my involvement in the healing ministry is that, more than anything else I know, it is a most effective means of proclaiming the good news of Christ and of the Holy Spirit. I have seen more people converted to Christ through the ministry of healing, than through any other form of outreach I myself have shared in. And I have seen more Christians enter into a deeper spiritual life through the laying on of hands for healing, than in any other way, as far as my experience goes.

When we stretch out our hands that the Lord may heal, when we pray the prayer of faith for healing, we are acting as channels for the power of the Holy Spirit. It is the Holy Spirit who quickens our bodies and those for whom we pray, and that is how healing takes place. But the scripture tells us that the Holy Spirit shows Christ to us. This is what the Holy Spirit *must* do, for that is his character. He is the Spirit of Christ. The first observation I made when I began the ministry of healing, was that people on whom hands were laid for healing prospered more in their experience of Jesus than those who did not receive this ministry.

In the years I have been involved in the healing ministry, I don't say that all those to whom we have ministered have been healed. A great number have been; a minority of them at once, the rest in a progressive way. But whether they have been healed or not, I am able to say without reservation that *there has not been one person in the whole of that time, who has been anything but thankful to Almighty God for the blessings he has received*, because to each and every person, the Holy Spirit has shown Jesus. And that is perfect blessing, for any eventuality in this life, and for the life to come. In this most important respect, the healing ministry *never* fails!

My last illustration is a testimony to what I am saying here. In this case the person concerned was *not* healed physically. I do not wish to give the impression that the healing ministry has no disappointments, because that isn't true.

A clergyman of another denomination once asked me to come with him and minister to a woman who was one of his church members. The woman had cancer, and medically speaking, had only a few weeks to live. I went with the minister to visit her, and found both her and her family in great distress. "Why should this have happened to us?" they were asking. It was clear that they just didn't know which way to turn in the midst of all their trouble. My heart always goes out to people in that situation.

The other clergyman and I laid hands on her and shared our vicarious faith with her. I went back several times, and her own minister went back many times as we continued to add faith to faith. Instead of living only a few weeks, she lived eighteen months, which in itself was remarkable. But then she died, and it was because of the cancer that she died. Yet in that eighteen months, she and all her family had come to know the Lord. They had the peace which passes understanding and the joy that no man takes away. So much so that, on the day she died, her husband sent a message to me through his minister, asking that "prayers of thanksgiving be publicly offered for all the blessings we have received."

I think that I should say a word in general here about those who are not healed. The first point is that there may well be weaknesses in our prayer that need to be recognised so that our ministry of healing is made more effective. We have referred to a number of matters that have to be taken into account and have tried to speak the truth in love.

Having said that, we all know of times when faith has been exercised in a truly scriptural way, but still healing has not resulted. In those circumstances we can only be reverently agnostic and say that we do not know why. If it is that they have died, we can only affirm in continuing faith: "The Lord gave, and the Lord has taken away; blessed be the name of the Lord."[10]

At such times as these in my own ministry I have noticed that two things regularly happen. The person's life is prolonged and during that time he or she draws on the blessing of Jesus in a way that is needful. It seems that by the exercise of our faith the Lord is enabled to keep them here until, through the ministry of the Holy Spirit, the things of eternity are understood and entered into, and then he takes them quietly to be with himself. Different people would have different testimonies to give at this point, but all would have a note of the miraculous about them. Surely there is healing in that too.

* * *

Our Lord came to preach the gospel and to heal the sick. That was also the work he sent his followers to do, and that is the on-going ministry which his servants are still called to fulfil in his name and for his sake. Yet by and large the church has left half of this commission behind, and then we wonder why the other half seems so ineffective. We fail to realise that if we disturb the "ecology" of God, the whole dynamic of God's blessing for his children will be altered and put out of gear.

For twenty years I have sought (with others) to act on the commission as given. I can only thank God that, despite my personal failings, it has been a story of continuous blessing. I have found that both halves of the commission complement each other so that a whole new dynamic of ministry comes into being, or rather is recovered.

The negative forebodings have not eventuated. "You'll be leading people up the garden path"... "What about if they are not healed? The faith they have will be adversely

affected..." etc. In fairness to some who have expressed these
views, I have to say that when they have seen help and not
hindrance coming through this ministry, they have done
what they could to support it in a practical way.

As a congregation, we of St Andrew's Cathedral healing
ministry, have the concept of being "The Holy Community."
It is a concept every congregation should have. Certainly we
have had our set-backs, but these have enabled us to depend
on God more, so that we are "straining forward to what lies
ahead."[11] We have a ministry of all believers that is unique in
my experience of church life. There is an increasing interdependence between all who are involved; a growing in unity,
love, vision, prayer and outreach.

All this has developed and is practised within the historic
church with its supportive fellowship and kindly discipline.
Such balance and maturity as we now have, come from
having to relate to the wider body and take into account the
standpoint of those who sometimes see things differently.
Those who are set in authority over us are patient, sympathe-
tic and encouraging. We, for our part, study to be loyal.

The prayer of the first Christians was: "Lord, grant to thy
servants to speak thy word with all boldness, while thou
stretchest out thy hand to heal, and signs and wonders are
performed through the name of thy holy servant Jesus."[12]
Because God is the same now as then, that prayer needs to be
ours if we are to fulfil God's will in our generation. It is
certainly the prayer and practice of those who are committed
to the healing ministry of the church.

A prayer
Father God, we thank you that you have given us the
wonderful privilege of making "intercessions for all men."
We know and rejoice that this is but a small reflection of the
intercession that Christ ever lives to make for us, and of the
intercession of the Holy Spirit that is "with sighs too deep
for words."

We praise you for those who have prayed for us over all the years and for whom we have prayed. Only you, O God, know all the blessing that those prayers have made possible. Our hearts are full of loving gratitude.

Father, we would take up our role of being intercessors. We believe for and with others; for conversion, for healing, for all that you provide and all that they need. We continue in prayer, rejoicing that by faith we can thank you for what we do not yet see.

O Father of all mankind, give us a vision of believing for the world for whom Christ died. We begin to believe for all men everywhere, especially for those who do not yet have faith themselves. Thank you for the blessing of Jesus which even now is flowing.

Glory be to the Father, and to the Son, and to the Holy Ghost; as it was in the beginning, is now and ever shall be, world without end!

Appendix to Part I

Guidelines for those who are receiving
medical treatment and who wish to draw
on the healing ministry

Continue to draw on the medical treatment as prescribed by the doctor and do it with a good conscience.

Tell the doctor that you are attending a service of divine healing and keep him informed as to the results.

Do not let the medical prognosis limit your faith expectation. Look past the treatment and prognosis to God and believe that with him all things are possible. Let that become the measure and reality of your faith.

Part II

Scriptural Understanding

7

Why did Christ Heal?

THE GOSPELS RECORD twenty-six cases of individual healings performed by Christ, and ten cases of multiple healings, ranging from a "few" to a "great multitude".[1] It was said of him that he went about "healing every disease and every infirmity among the people;"[2] that "as many as touched it (his garment) were made well;"[3] and that he healed "all that were oppressed by the devil."[4]

If we ask why Christ performed these healings we find, if we look at them, that a number of reasons are given. One reason will be given for one healing and another reason will be given for another. If a balanced scriptural understanding is to be reached, every healing has to be examined so that all the reasons are seen and put together.

One reason given was that our Lord saw his acts of healing as an expression of the mind and will of God. In the case of the healing of the man born blind, he said, "We must work the works of him who sent me."[5] To the leper who said, "If you will, you can make me clean," he replied, "I will; be clean."[6] More generally, he said, "My food is to do the will of him who sent me and to accomplish his work."[7]

They were also a sign of his compassion. Sometimes with an individual: "Moved with pity, he stretched out his hand and touched him...and immediately the leprosy left him."[8]

And sometimes with a crowd: "He saw a great throng; and he had compassion on them, and healed their sick."[9]

Healing was also a fulfilment of prophecy. "He cast out the spirits with a word, and healed all who were sick. This was to fulfil what was spoken by the prophet Isaiah, 'He took our infirmities and bore our diseases.'"[10] This prophecy comes from the suffering servant passage in Isaiah chapter 53 and in the view of some can only mean that healing is included in the atonement.

Our Lord was never concerned that his emphasis on healing, with the huge public response it evoked, might distract from his primary concern for the salvation of the soul. On the contrary, Jesus often used these manifestations of divine power to draw attention to himself and to his work of redemption.

This was illustrated in the account of the paralytic brought to him by friends.[11] Before healing him, Jesus told him that his sins were forgiven. To the protests that followed, and to the accusation of blasphemy, our Lord replied that the healing miracle he was about to perform was the proof of his power to forgive sins, confirming that he was indeed the Son of God, the long-awaited Messiah. This reason for healing was again seen when the disciples of John the Baptist came and asked him, "Are you he who is to come, or shall we look for another?" And he replied, "Go and tell John what you hear and see: the blind receive their sight and the lame walk, lepers are cleansed and the deaf hear, and the dead are raised up, and the poor have good news preached to them."[12]

There were other occasions when Jesus used sickness and healing to glorify God. In the case of Lazarus, he explained to his disciples, "This illness is not unto death; it is for the glory of God, so that the Son of God may be glorified by means of it."[13] Speaking of the man born blind he declared: "It was not that this man sinned, or his parents, but that the works of God might be made manifest in him."[14]

Sometimes Jesus used healing to stimulate faith, as in this case of the man born blind. Having sent the man to the pool of Siloam, where he was healed, Jesus later met him and asked, "Do you believe in the son of man?" He answered, "And who is he, sir, that I may believe in him?" Jesus said to him, "You have seen him and it is he who speaks to you." He said, "Lord, I believe;"[15] and he worshipped him. The same point was made when he said to Philip, "Believe me that I am in the Father and the Father in me; or else believe me for the sake of the works themselves."[16]

When people came to Christ for healing he responded, more often than not without any comment about spiritual things. He never said, "I am willing to heal you, but you must realise there is something more important." Even when Jesus emphasised the spiritual work of redemption, he never did so in any way that minimised the importance of physical healing. What concerned him was the faith of the person making the request, whether the healing was for himself or for someone else.

Faith in Christ for healing

A study of our Lord's healings reveals that nearly always he asked the sick to have faith that he would heal.

"Two blind men followed him, crying aloud, 'Have mercy on us, son of David.' Jesus said to them, 'Do you believe that I am able to do this?' They said to him, 'Yes, Lord.' Then he touched their eyes, saying, 'According to your faith be it done to you.' And their eyes were opened."[17]

We see the role of faith again in the case of the woman who had been sick with an issue of blood for twelve years. She approached to touch his garment because "she had heard about him." When Jesus singled her out of the crowd and she fell down before him, he said to her, "Daughter, your faith has made you well; go in peace, and be healed of your disease."[18] Further examples are the case of the Centurion of

Capernaum[19] when Jesus marvelled at finding such faith, and the raising of Jairus' daughter.[20]

The necessity for faith in Jesus' capacity to heal was brought home conclusively by what happened, or indeed by what failed to happen, when faith was lacking. The unbelief of the inhabitants of Nazareth in his divine mission prompted Jesus to declare, "A prophet is not without honour except in his own country, and in his own house."[21] These very significant words then follow, "And he did not do many mighty works/ could do no mighty work/ there, because of their unbelief."[22][23]

These and many other instances show that one of the essential elements in our Lord's acts of healing, was faith in him to heal. It was a reason why he healed, and where it was lacking, it was the reason why he did *not* heal.

The dynamic of healing

As we have already seen, Christ healed because it was God's will; he healed because of his compassion; he healed to fulfil prophecy; he healed to confirm his Messiahship and his power to forgive sins; he healed to give glory to God; he healed to bring people to believe in him as Lord; and he healed in response to faith.

But there is more to be said than this. The curse which followed the fall of man exposed man to sickness, suffering and death. The serpent caused the fall; the fall caused sickness; "...the devil has sinned from the beginning. The reason the Son of God appeared was to destroy the works of the devil."[24] The gospels provide ample evidence that, as far as Jesus was concerned, sickness was the work of Satan.

This was shown in the case of the Gadarene demoniac[25] "who had demons", or with a "blind and dumb demoniac".[26] Thus, whether the problem was "devil possession sickness", or physical sickness in general, Jesus looked upon it as being the work of Satan. This could be thought of either as "a devil", or the work of Satan as seen in the sin of the world.

When the ruler of the synagogue expressed his indignation that the Lord had healed a woman on the sabbath day, Jesus retorted, "Ought not this woman, whom Satan bound for eighteen years, be loosed from this bond on the sabbath day?"[27] The sabbath day for the chosen people was the day commemorating the fulfilment of divine creation, good and perfect. But the woman's sickness was bondage to Satan, and thus formed no part of God's good and perfect will for her.

When the pharisees accused Jesus of casting out devils (a blind and dumb demoniac) by Beelzebub the prince of devils, he replied that it was impossible to cast out Satan by Satan; for then Satan would be divided against himself and his kingdom would not stand. This is saying in effect that healing is acting on behalf of God "to destroy the works of the devil." It is part of the restoring work of God, which is what salvation is all about.

The positive corollary of destroying the works of the devil is extending the kingdom of God. This latter is commonly taken to mean that the rule of Christ is extended in the lives of people. There is, of course, no disagreement with that as far as it goes. The kingdom obviously has kingship as its cornerstone. But it is not kingship only. If it is, that is the way it would have been referred to in the gospels; but Christ in his very many references to it, spoke of it as "the kingdom," and specified what he meant by that. Let us look at the principal things he said.

The kingdom of God

Our Lord revealed that the kingdom is both eschatological and contemporary. It belongs to the end of the age, as well as being present with us now. These are different aspects of the truth and have to be put together if the revelation is to be seen in fullness and balance. Frequently Jesus said more than one thing about a particular matter, and these insights appear in different places. The definitive text is not one or the other, but both or all.

Part of what he revealed about the kingdom of God is that it is a heavenly or spiritual reality and will not be experienced in perfection until "the kingdom of the world has become the kingdom of our Lord and of his Christ."[28] Then "death shall be no more, neither shall there be mourning nor crying nor pain any more, for the former things have passed away."[29] This reality of the kingdom belongs to the future, just as some of the other promises of God belong to the future.

Jesus also affirmed that the kingdom had already been established. "Being asked by the Pharisees when the kingdom of God was coming, he answered them, 'The kingdom of God is not coming with signs to be observed; nor will they say, "Look here it is!" or "There!" for behold, the kingdom of God is in the midst of you.'"[30] To the question, "What is the kingdom of God like?" Jesus answered, "It is like a grain of mustard seed which a man took and sowed in his garden; and it grew and became a tree. Again...it is like leaven which a woman took and hid in three measures of flour, till it was all leavened."[31] He said it would develop, not by apocalyptic interference, but as grain grows — "first the blade, then the ear, then the full grain in the ear."[32]

So the kingdom is here and it is growing. We have every reason therefore to expect to see the signs of the kingdom — the first fruits of what is to come. The signs that will be seen now, can only be those that were seen at the beginning. The same kingdom will have the same signs. This does not preclude a future coming of the kingdom with power and glory at the time of the second advent when *all* the signs will be seen. The growing kingdom will then become the consummated kingdom.

Our Lord clearly stated that one of the signs of the kingdom-in-the-midst-of-us is healing. This is what is meant when he said, "If it is by the spirit of God that I cast out demons, then the kingdom of God has come upon you."[33] When he said to the general group of disciples, "Heal the sick and say to them, 'The kingdom of God has come near to you,'"[34] he said the same thing, but with the added information that this was true as much for their ministry as for his.

Other signs of the present reality of the kingdom are the things that we eat, drink and wear. "Seek his kingdom, and these things shall be yours as well,"[35*] we are told. It was in regard to the signs that are to be seen now that Christ stressed the availability of the kingdom: "Fear not, little flock, for it is your Father's good pleasure to give you the kingdom."[36]

This means that the signs of the kingdom that are to be seen now are the kingship of Christ, the resource of divine healing, and the provision of our material needs. Because the reality of the kingdom of which they are manifestations has been given to us so that it is in our midst, these blessings are available now and only wait to be appropriated by repentance, faith and obedience.

As well as these signs being an *expression* of the kingdom, they are also an *extension* of the kingdom. When "the works of the devil" are destroyed and "the kingdom of God has come," it can only mean that the kingdom has been extended in that

*Footnote

The statement in Romans 14:17 that "the kingdom of God is not food and drink but righteousness and peace and joy in the Holy Spirit" has to be understood in its context. It stemmed from a local controversy over eating meat that had been offered to idols. Paul said that there was nothing wrong with this, but if it caused offence to someone who believed it was wrong, it should be avoided. For after all, he said, the important thing is not what we eat and drink, but stirring up righteousness in the Holy Spirit. Obviously this does not cut across what Christ has said, that as we seek the kingdom, what is needed in food and drink will be added to us.

way and in that degree. When we speak about "extending the kingdom of God", it refers to *all* the signs that are to be seen now and not the kingship of Christ only. The ultimate reason why Christ healed was to extend the kingdom of God. Healing was only part of that work, but it *was* part and it was an *essential* part.

*   *   *

This study of our Lord's healing ministry shows that there were a number of reasons why he healed. They are all valid and relevant and together make up the whole. One cannot take one of the reasons, however important it happens to be, (such as healing being used to validate his power to forgive sins) and say that was the definitive reason why Christ healed. The Bible says nothing to justify such a conclusion. Neither does it say that one reason was more important than another. On the contrary each reason stands in its own right and serves its own purpose.

Some reasons for healing were personal to Christ and demonstrated that he was the long awaited Messiah who had the power to forgive sins. These personal reasons glorified him as the Son of God and brought people to believe in him as Lord. They also showed that in healing he "took our infirmities and bore our diseases," so that Peter could say, "by his wounds you have been healed."[37]

Other reasons clearly showed that healing was part of Christ's overall work of destroying the works of the devil and extending the kingdom of God. This was the inner dynamic of healing and the only requirement was faith. These reasons for Christ's healings were not personal to him alone but were, he said, to be the ministry that he and his disciples would have in common.[38]

We therefore conclude that the reasons that were personal to Christ do not in any way preclude other reasons for his healing, which equally applied to his followers, and were the reasons why they would heal in the same way as did he.

With this in mind, let us now look at what the New Testament has to say about the involvement of others in divine healing.

8

The Healing Ministry of the Disciples

IT IS OBVIOUS that our Lord did not look upon the healing ministry as being unique to himself because he committed the same ministry to his followers. His instruction in and promise of this are found no less than five times in the gospels.[1]

Jesus gave the twelve "authority over unclean spirits, to cast them out, and to heal every disease and every infirmity."[2] "He sent them out to preach the kingdom of God and to heal."[3] And this is what they did. "They went out and preached that men should repent. And they cast out many demons, and anointed with oil many that were sick and healed them."[4] "And they departed and went through the villages, preaching the gospel and healing everywhere."[5]

Neither was this healing ministry limited to the apostles. The same call and commission was given to the wider and more general circle of the seventy disciples. "Whenever you enter a town and they receive you...heal the sick in it and say to them, 'the kingdom of God has come near to you.'"[6] The same group subsequently reported, "Lord, even the demons are subject to us in your name!" And Jesus replied: "I saw Satan fall like lightning from heaven. Behold, I have given you authority to tread upon serpents and scorpions, and over all the power of the enemy; and nothing shall hurt you. Nevertheless do not rejoice in this, that the spirits are subject to you; but rejoice that your names are written in heaven."[7]

It is of value to make a comparative study of the commissions to the twelve and to the seventy, because it shows that they are essentially the same. In some places, in fact, they are word for word.

The Twelve[8] [9]

He called to him his twelve disciples and gave them authority over unclean spirits, to cast them out, and to heal every disease and every infirmity. These twelve Jesus sent out two by two, charging them, "Go nowhere among the Gentiles, and enter no town of the Samaritans, but go rather to the lost sheep of the house of Israel. And preach as you go, saying, 'The kingdom of heaven is at hand.' Heal the sick, raise the dead, cleanse lepers, cast out demons. You have received without paying, give without pay. Take no gold, nor silver, nor copper in your belts, no bag for your journey, nor two tunics, nor sandals, nor a staff; for the labourer deserves his food. And whatever town or village you enter, find out

The Seventy[10]

The Lord appointed seventy others and sent them on ahead of him, two by two, into every town and place where he himself was about to come. And he said to them, "The harvest is plentiful, but the labourers are few; pray therefore the Lord of the harvest to send out labourers into his harvest.

Heal the sick...and say to them 'The kingdom of God has come near to you.'

Carry no purse,
no bag,

no sandals; for the labourer deserves his wages. Whenever you enter a town and they receive you, eat what is who is worthy in it, and stay with him until you depart. As you enter the house, salute it. And if the house is worthy, let your peace come upon it; but if it is not worthy let your peace return to you.

And if anyone will not receive you,...shake off the dust from your feet as you leave that house or town.

I say to you, it shall be more tolerable on the day of judgment for...Sodom and Gomorrah than for that town.

Behold, I send you out as sheep in the midst of wolves..."

set before you. Whatever house you enter, first say, 'Peace be to this house.' And if a son of peace is there, your peace shall rest upon him; but if not, it shall return to you.

But whenever you enter a town and they do not receive you,...say, 'Even the dust of your town that clings to our feet, we wipe off against you.'

I tell you, it shall be more tolerable on that day for Sodom than for that town.

Behold, I send you out as lambs in the midst of wolves..."

This comparison demonstrates quite clearly that all the disciples of the Lord were instructed to act in the same way, which was the way in which the Lord himself acted. The apostles were to do the same as did the Lord, and the seventy were to do the same as the apostles. They knew they had a personal responsibility to discharge in healing the sick. It was done by faith and it was done in the name of Christ. It was linked with the commission to preach repentance and the kingdom of God.[11] Evangelism and healing were to go hand in hand; healing was to be as normal a ministry as preaching the word; they were spoken of and practised together. The followers of Christ were never sent out to preach but that they were also sent out to heal.

In the long ending to St Mark's gospel,[12] our Lord is

recorded as saying, "And these signs will accompany those who believe...they will lay their hands on the sick, and they will recover." It needs to be said that these verses are not found in the oldest and best Greek manuscripts. Theologians generally believe the original ending to the gospel was lost, and that what we have here is an attempt to reconstruct a conclusion. Written at the end of the first century, or the beginning of the second, it is composed from other known sayings of Christ,[13] as well as from what was recorded in Acts.[14]

At least it is a very early statement which reflects what the first Christians understood and practised. This in itself is an exceedingly valuable piece of information, because what we are seeking to do in this whole exercise is to have a right perspective of what the Bible says about healing. Thus, if we can get close to those who were themselves close to Christ and his immediate followers, and see what perspective *they* had about these matters, it will make a valuable and even unique contribution to the understanding that *we* should have. And this is what they affirmed as the truth of the matter, "Those who believe...will lay their hands on the sick, and they will recover."

The healing ministry of the disciples recorded in Acts

The book of the Acts of the Apostles records nine cases of individual healings by the disciples, and refers to multiple healings on seven occasions.

The individual cases are: the paralytic at the Beautiful Gate;[15] Paul's sight recovered;[16] Aeneas healed of paralysis;[17] Tabitha restored to life;[18] the crippled man at Lystra being made to walk again;[19] a girl freed from a spirit of divination;[20] Eutychus brought back to life;[21] Paul unharmed by the bite of a viper;[22] and the father of Publius healed of fever and dysentery.[23]

The multiple healings are recorded firstly in chapter 2: 43, "...many wonders and signs were done through the apostles."

Much the same thing is said again in chapter 5: 12-16. Then, "Stephen, full of grace and power did great wonders and signs among the people."[24] Philip also healed many sick people.[25] Signs and wonders were done by the hands of Paul and Barnabas.[26] At Ephesus, God wrought special miracles by the hands of Paul.[27] And, on the island of Malta, those who had diseases came and were healed.[28]

One can only marvel at the simple affirmation of Peter to Aeneas the paralytic, "Aeneas, Jesus Christ heals you; rise and make your bed."[29] Where did Peter gain this certainty that, in the particular case of Aeneas, Jesus Christ wanted to heal him? Either Peter believed the will of the Lord was always to heal, or he received a direct revelation from the Holy Spirit that Aeneas was to be the object of a striking manifestation of divine power. But no mention is made of any such revelation in Acts or elsewhere. If one relies on the scriptures for an explanation, one can only fall back on the command and commission of Christ, and the conviction of the apostles and disciples generally, that, as they stretched out their hands to heal, God would raise up the sick. They clearly felt at liberty to affirm that healing would result from faith — either their own faith or the faith of the one who was sick.[30]

It is important to note that the apostles always disowned the idea that healing was something given personally to them as apostles. After the healing of the paralytic at the Beautiful Gate, Peter declared that there was no reason why the people should marvel at such a miracle "as though by our own power or piety we had made him walk."[31] Peter diverted all attention from himself as the instrument, directing it to him who was the author of the manifestation. "And his name, by faith in his name, has made this man strong whom you see and know; and the faith which is through Jesus has given the man this perfect health in the presence of you all." Peter had simply said to the man, "In the name of Jesus Christ of Nazareth, walk."[31] The circumstances of Paul's healing of the cripple at Lystra are noticeably similar.[32]

Although the deacons were not commissioned as such to preach and heal, it is clear that Philip and Stephen had extensive ministries in these areas, not less in their content and effect than those of the apostles. Healing is not specifically mentioned in regard to Stephen's ministry, but he "did great wonders and signs among the people."[33] The word "signs" in this context is the same word as that used to describe the healing ministry of Philip: "...they...saw the signs which he did. For unclean spirits came out of many who were possessed, crying with a loud voice; and many who were paralysed or lame were healed."[34] It thus seems most likely that Stephen healed, but if this is unacceptable, the comment on healing could be confined to Philip.

The wide practice of the healing ministry in the early church is further shown by the ministry of Barnabas, who was neither of the twelve nor the seventy, but of whom it was said, with Paul: "...the Lord...granting signs and wonders to be done by their hands."[35] There was also the case of Ananias, who laid hands on Paul in order that he would recover his sight.[36]

From this review, it could be said that no specific commission to preach and heal was regarded as necessary in the early church. Its members were all witnesses and they all had a ministry, and healing was an essential part of their witness and ministry. Alternatively, the commission to the seventy disciples, with its on-going authority,[37] could have been understood as a general commission to all disciples. Again, it is possible that the commission recorded in Mark 16: 17-18 was authentic and that it was acted upon.

The fact that healing was practised in the early church in a wide and on-going variety of circumstances is an obvious conclusion. To say, as some do, that it was associated with particular events that gave it a unique and not to be repeated significance, is to make a far-reaching assertion for which there is not one word of justification in the scriptures. On the contrary, the almost casual way in which the various instances of healing are recorded in the narrative shows that it was looked upon as a normal every-day occurrence, as well as a living reality that was never in doubt.

9

The Gifts of Healing and James 5: 14,15

The gifts of healing

IN 1 CORINTHIANS 12, PAUL said that the Holy Spirit divides his ministries among Christian believers, and one of those ministries is healing. He further explains that not everyone will have the same gift ministry, but everyone is intended to have some gift. Some Christians will therefore have the gift of healing.

This raises the question: does this mean that only certain 'gifted' people will be involved in the healing ministry? How is this reconciled with the statement that "those who believe will lay their hands on the sick?"[1] The answer is seen if we look at another gift of the Spirit — the gift of faith. Do only certain people have faith? The answer to this question is "no," because the Bible says that "without faith it is impossible to please him."[2] Every Christian has faith, but some have a special ministry in that area. The same applies to healing and all the gifts. Every Christian can share in the healing ministry, but some Christians will have a special calling to that work.

The general point made by St Paul is that one of the ways that healing is manifest in the on-going church is through a special ministry of healing that is given to certain individuals. This will complement the general involvement of Christians in healing as it will complement the other ministries given by the Spirit.

James 5: 14,15

The passage in James 5: 14,15 sets out, in a church orientated way, what has been previously said in terms of itinerant preaching healing ministries. As such, it provides special insights into the church's ministry of healing for today. It is a valuable confirmation of what has been previously recorded in the New Testament, and shows plainly that the established and local church was expected to heal as well as to preach.

"Is any among you sick? Let him call for the elders of the church, and let them pray over him, anointing him with oil in the name of the Lord; and the prayer of faith will save the sick man, and the Lord will raise him up; and if he has committed sins, he will be forgiven."

In response to the sick person's call, the elders of the church are to anoint him and pray the prayer of faith. This prayer of faith will make operative three promises: the sick person shall be saved; the Lord shall raise him up; and he shall be forgiven his sins. It is clear that, while the presenting circumstances are to do with sickness, and there is the obvious need to do something effective about them, the provision and response of God cover the whole range of salvation. The sick person is to be saved, healed and forgiven.

This means that the healing ministry of the church is concerned with people being made whole. As well as the immediate problem there is the need to deal with the deep underlying causative factors. As well as the body there is the need for the mind to be healed, and not only the body and mind, but also the spirit. There is the need for the soul to be reconciled to God through Christ. This also shows how truly evangelistic the healing ministry is. It begins at the point of felt need and leads on to the deep and eternal things of the faith. Where it is followed through with that understanding, that is exactly what happens.

James 5: 14,15 is not in any way an isolated text. This can be seen if it is looked at in its New Testament context. Healing was first explained in much detail by the Lord himself in the gospels. The commission to heal in the same way was then given to the twelve and the seventy. (The equivalent of that today would be the elders and the general members of the congregation.) The understanding of the first Christians was that this commission was to "those who believe". The deacons, for example, were not set apart to preach and heal, but two of them, at least, had a ministry in these areas like that of the apostles. This means that there was a general commission, or that a commission was not necessary. Paul stated that gifts of healing are part of the ministry of the Holy Spirit, and finally, as we have just seen, James set out healing in pastoral terms for the on-going church, linking it intimately with salvation.

The James passage is part of this consistent New Testament revelation and is to be understood in that setting. It enhances what has been said earlier by showing that it is applicable today. It adds to the revelation by saying that healing is to be exercised in the local church and by giving a detailed blueprint to follow. It is a logical development of all that has gone before and is a natural conclusion.

10

Four Common Objections

The value of suffering

IT IS OFTEN SAID that there is "value in suffering". It is assumed that suffering includes sickness, so the next step is to reason that it may not be God's will for us to be healed and this means that we need to conclude our prayer with the phrase "if it be thy will".

But is this the right understanding of the matter? Obviously, the first requirement is to avoid making any uncritical assumptions. Our only guide is what God has revealed to us in his written word. We need to be quite clear in our minds concerning the meaning of words or concepts in the Bible. We must also know what they do not mean. To reach this understanding, it is necessary for us to examine all the relevant passages to see the meaning in each case, and whether or not there is the same meaning in every case. We should also be concerned to find broad and consistent themes. We are not to build a line of thought on an isolated text, and conversely, we are not to set aside a broad and consistent theme because of an isolated text. What, then, does the Bible reveal to us about suffering?

It was said of Christ, "Although he was a Son, he learned obedience through what he suffered."[1] If we ask in what way Christ "suffered," we find the answer in Matthew 16:21:

"Jesus began to show his disciples that he must go to Jerusalem and suffer many things from the elders and chief priests and scribes, and be killed, and on the third day be raised." Luke in 24:46 said the same thing: "Thus it is written, that the Christ should suffer and on the third day rise from the dead."

The suffering of Christ was to do with his atonement. Through his suffering he learned obedience to his Father's will, "and being made perfect he became the source of eternal salvation to all who obey him."[2] It was not a reference to sickness; Jesus suffered, but he was not sick.

When it comes to the suffering experienced by the followers of Christ, we read in 2 Corinthians 1:5 that "we share abundantly in Christ's sufferings." We know that this does not mean we share in the suffering of our Lord's atonement, but the meaning becomes clear as we examine and compare other references. The apostles rejoiced "that they were counted worthy to suffer dishonour for the name."[3] Peter said, "Even if you do suffer for righteousness' sake...for doing right."[4] To the Thessalonians Paul said, "You suffered the same things from your own countrymen as they did from the Jews."[5] Of St Paul and his sufferings Jesus said, "He is a chosen instrument of mine to carry my name before the Gentiles and kings and the sons of Israel; for I will show him how much he must suffer for the sake of my name."[6]

The meaning of "suffering" in the New Testament, as far as the Christian is concerned, is the persecution that comes from being a Christian. This is the broad and consistent theme and there are no exceptions. There are other meanings to the word "suffer," such as "to hold up," "to permit," etc., but they do not affect the issue. As with the suffering of Christ, the use of the word in relation to the Christian is not in any way a reference to sickness.

In 2 Corinthians 1: 8,9, Paul explained that suffering has a redemptive purpose: "We do not want you to be ignorant, brethren, of the affliction we experienced in Asia; for we were so utterly, unbearably crushed that we despaired of life itself. Why, we felt that we had received the sentence of death; but that was to make us rely not on ourselves but on God who raises the dead." Paul's difficulties brought him "to the end of his tether," (Phillips) so that he had to trust, not in his fallen self-nature, but wholly in God. When the Christian experiences this he is also learning obedience to the Father's will, for "a servant is not greater than his master."[7]

But when we come to consider what the New Testament says about sickness, the picture is as different as it is distinct. Sickness is always sickness; it is never described as suffering. And we are to react to it quite differently. We have already seen that the only requirement was faith that Christ would heal. "According to your faith, be it done to you," he said. Here again there is a broad and consistent theme. Where healing did not eventuate, either as in the case of the disciples who failed to heal the boy, or as with the inhabitants of Nazareth, it was because of "little faith" and "unbelief."

Nowhere in the New Testament is sickness shown to be suffering which is beneficial. Should anyone wish to say that experience today shows there is value in sickness, one could reply that there was the same value in it to all who sought healing in the Scripture narratives, yet this aspect was never so much as mentioned. Nowhere did it limit the availability of healing in response to faith.

Thus, the meaning of "suffering" in the New Testament is always "for being a Christian;" it never means "being sick." Anyone who confuses the two is ignoring the obvious difference and distinction that the scriptures make. Suffering for the Christian is intended to be a redemptive experience by which we learn the obedience of trusting not in ourselves, but in God. This is the value of suffering, and its importance cannot be overstressed. Nowhere does the New Testament speak of "sickness" in the same way. "Suffering" is to be redemptive; "sickness" is to be healed.

St James set it out clearly when he said, "Is any one among

you suffering? Let him pray...Is any among you sick? Let him call for the elders of the church."[8] He saw them as different matters and said that we are to react to them in different ways.

Paul's thorn

This is the illustration from the New Testament which is so often used to maintain that it may not be God's will to heal. If God did not heal St Paul, who prayed three times that his "thorn in the flesh"[9] be taken from him, and to whom God said, "My grace is sufficient for you," then he might not will to heal us. If so, we have to pray, "if it be thy will".

If this understanding of Paul's thorn is correct, then we must accept it. But we must be quite certain about it, because, if true, it qualifies our Lord's teaching and practice that only faith was needed for healing. Likewise the teaching and practice of Paul himself, who saw that the cripple "had faith to be made well".[10] It is no light matter to compromise what Christ himself said and taught. If, on the other hand, our enquiry shows the common understanding of Paul's thorn to be no more than a tradition of man, we have a clear duty to expose that fallacy and to reject it. So, because a correct understanding of the "thorn" is vital to a right exposition of healing, it is necessary to deal with it in some detail.

Let us begin by giving the "thorn" its full and alleged significance; let us assume it was a sickness, and that it was not God's will to heal the apostle. Thus, in spite of what Christ and the rest of the New Testament affirm, we now have one instance where healing was *not* available in response to faith. So at this point, the question we need to ask is: does one exception set aside what is otherwise the rule, so that there is no longer any rule to apply? By "the rule", we mean what the rest of the evidence obviously shows to be the truth of the matter. By "the exception", we mean a single circumstance where this does not apply. It has been said that only a single genuine exception has to be found for a rule to be no longer a rule.

But is this really an acceptable view? In other disciplines, in physics for example, "the exception proves (or illustrates) the rule." If there is an exception to the general rule, it is an exception, and the rule stands as the general norm. To argue then from the apparent exception to a denial of the rule is illogical and unfounded. And in this case, it makes what Christ has said to count for nothing! Surely it is what the New Testament says as a whole that is the important point. So, assuming for the moment that Paul's thorn was an exception, that fact does not affect at all the general rule of healing as otherwise revealed in the New Testament.

But we are not even sure that it was an exception. From the context of 2 Corinthians 11:21-12:10, we do not know what Paul was referring to when he speaks of being given "a thorn in the flesh". It is not simply that we do not know what *kind* of sickness he had; we do not know if it *was* a sickness. It has been assumed it was a sickness because it is described as "a thorn in *the flesh*". The assumption is then taken as fact, so that the only speculation remaining is what form the sickness took.

Taking our enquiry a step further, let us now refer back to what we call the Old Testament, but which to Paul was "the scriptures," and see what "a thorn" meant to his scriptural understanding. In the Old Testament, "thorns" were used as a figure of speech, and always referred to people, never to things or conditions. "The inhabitants of the land...shall be as pricks in your eyes and thorns in your sides...[11] They shall be a scourge on your sides, and thorns in your eyes."[12] Obviously these statements meant that people, described as "thorns in your sides," were going to be very hurtful. "Thorns" in Paul's understanding of the scriptures were always people; they were never sicknesses or the spirits of sickness.

When we come to his own use of the phrase, we see, as we

might expect from this background of understanding, that it stands for a person. "A thorn was given me in the flesh, *a messenger of Satan*."[13] In the original Greek, the word "messenger" is "aggelos", which appears 188 times in the New Testament. It is translated 181 times as "angel", and in seven cases as "messenger". It is always translated as a person, never as an object, and it has no connection with sickness.

The straightforward interpretation of what Paul wrote is that a messenger (a person) of Satan was a thorn in the flesh to him. The thorn in the flesh was a figurative way of describing a messenger or angel of Satan who continually harassed him — in much the same way as we say that someone is "a pain in the neck". No one would ever think that a person referred to in this way was literally causing a pain in the neck. Everyone knows what is meant to the point where an explanation is hardly necessary — the person is a real annoyance — he or she is like "a pain in the neck".

To regard the "thorn" as a sickness is to impart to it a meaning which the Old Testament use of the word does not contain, and to ignore the meaning which is plainly employed. For there is a positive identification of the "thorn" with a person, both in the Old Testament, and in Paul's own explanation of what he meant. Among those who have identified the thorn with a person are Chrysostom, who noted it in his commentaries on the Epistles to the Corinthians, and Augustine of Hippo.

At this point we need take into account Paul's statement that the "thorn" and the consequent "weaknesses" were a redemptive experience for him. He rejoiced that he had been made weak in himself, so that he was strong in the Lord. As there is no reason to think the "thorn" was a sickness, this further identifies it with the "suffering" syndrome. The context is plainly what we have come to see suffering to be, as distinct from sickness. Paul said, "For the sake of Christ, then, I am content with weaknesses, insults, hardships, persecutions and calamities."[14] The only logical deduction from this is that the thorn and the resulting weaknesses were part of the suffering that came from his apostleship. This dovetails perfectly with our Lord's prophecy that in the course of carrying Christ's name before the Gentiles and kings and the sons of Israel, Paul would suffer greatly for his name's sake.

But irrespective of what the "thorn" was, the unique circumstances which led to Paul having this visitation make it most difficult to apply his experience in a general way. It is implied that Paul was caught up into the third heaven and heard unspeakable words. Because of that, he goes on to say, "To keep me from being too elated by the abundance of revelations, a thorn was given me in the flesh, a messenger of Satan..."[15] Doubtless it was this "abundance of revelations" that enabled Paul to discharge his responsibilities as the Apostle to the Gentiles, and provided the content of his epistles.

Christians today do not remotely correspond to these unique experiences and responsibilities. If the circumstances which led to Paul's thorn and prevented its removal do not apply to us, this scripture cannot logically be used to assert that because God did not remove Paul's thorn, he may not will to remove "a thorn" from us. Again this is irrespective of what the thorn was. Theologians strongly and rightly hold that one cannot make a general application from a unique premise.

Once Paul's thorn is seen in its full perspective, it cannot rightly be used to weaken the rule of healing as revealed by Christ. At most, it is an exception to the rule. Furthermore, an assumption has to be made that it was a sickness. The background scriptural use of the word has no connection with sickness; on the contrary, it is positively identified with persons. Paul uses it in the same sense. The facts that Paul said it was a redemptive experience, and that the context is that of persecution which fulfilled our Lord's prophecy concerning him, obviously identifies the problem with suffering as it is defined in the New Testament. In any case, the circumstances which led to the thorn and which prevented its removal were obviously unique to Paul, and therefore cannot be applied generally to others.

To use such an exception to set aside the unequivocal teaching of the Lord Jesus Christ, as well as the otherwise unanimous record of the New Testament, cannot be regarded as sound and reasonable biblical exegesis. The many who do this would not dream of expounding any other subject in the same way. Rather, they would be the first to point out the untheological and unacceptable nature of such an approach. Yet it is Paul's thorn, and Paul's thorn only, that is used to discount the dependability of healing in response to faith!

Notwithstanding what has been argued so far, the traditional approach should be reckoned with in its strongest form. For that reason we would accept that it is possible for a "messenger of Satan", in the shape of sickness, not to be removed by God. But by the same token, we require that the accompanying scriptural detail must be followed through as well. The proposition must be taken as a whole and not fragmented to suit the prejudice of the user. This means that if the person is not to be healed, this fact will be revealed by God. It also means that, up to this point, the prayer of faith will be acted upon in full expectancy of healing. Furthermore, if it is then revealed that healing is not to take place, it means that the sick person will "all the more gladly boast of (his or her) weaknesses,"[16] as did St Paul, and will not continue to seek their removal.

It is not good enough for someone to say that he is acting this out, just because a medical or prayer resource is not available to meet his particular need. If a medical development subsequently occurred that would enable him to be cured, would he not make use of it immediately? In such a case the argument for St Paul and his thorn would be very promptly forgotten!

So let those who maintain that Paul's thorn was a sickness, and applicable to us, apply it fully and honestly or not at all.

The fact that no one would think of applying this scripture in practice shows again how irrelevant it is to our circumstances, as well as how irrelevant it is to the exposition of healing.

This examination of Paul's thorn surely shows that the traditional interpretation has to be soundly rejected. If we accept, as we should, our Lord's teaching as primary, we will not expect to find anything in the rest of the New Testament to discount it. Thus we should hardly be surprised that the "thorn" objection does not stand investigation, and that what Christ revealed remains unquestioned and uncompromised. What *is* surprising is that the Christian church in the main has accepted this objection without critical enquiry, and has been content to set aside the teaching of our Lord!

Trophimus, Timothy and Epaphroditus

Paul had left Trophimus "ill at Miletus",[17] and he refers to Timothy's "frequent ailments".[18] Epaphroditus had been "ill, near to death",[19] but he was now recovered, and Paul was sending him to those who had been distressed by his illness, that they "may rejoice at seeing him again".[19] It is argued by some that if healing was available in response to faith, then surely Paul would have healed his companions.

It is possible that he did heal Epaphroditus; he certainly says that he recovered because "God had mercy on him".[19] If Epaphroditus was the only one to be considered, no reasonable person would bring him forward as a reason for maintaining that healing was not available in response to faith. The only case that can be made out is in respect to Trophimus and Timothy, who were sick at the time of Paul's writing. So let us consider these two.

If Paul had said that these two men were not converted at the time he was writing, would we conclude that it may not be God's will for all men to be saved? Of course not! We would make a judgement on the matter in the light of what the Bible otherwise said. And as the Bible says it is God's desire that all men should be saved,[20] we would assume there was some deficiency on their part, or on the part of their spiritual advisers, which had prevented them from appropriating this blessing. It would not occur to us to compromise what the Bible otherwise said, merely because we read that there were two men in need of salvation and who, at the time when Paul wrote, were not saved.

By using the same reasonable approach to make a judgement on the validity of healing in this situation, we would have to say that the Bible makes an express promise that the prayer of faith will save the sick man and the Lord will raise him up. We would also have to say that the New Testament testimony is wholly consistent on this matter. As a possible explanation of the difficulty, we would refer to another occasion where the disciples had actually attempted to heal someone and failed, and the Lord had stated that the hindrance was their "little faith".[21] When this was made good by his own perfect faith, the person concerned was immediately healed. Our Lord then explained that this was a deeper problem needing sacrificial prayer — showing, incidentally, that there is a quantitative aspect to faith.

Healing, like forgiveness, has to be drawn upon by faith and it can be difficult to believe for healing effectively. There is nothing to say that Trophimus and Timothy had been prayed for, and there is nothing to say they were not subsequently healed. (At any one time there are many who are sick and who are later healed, just as there are many unconverted who are later converted.)

Thus, to deduce that healing is not available in response to faith, merely because two persons happened to be sick at a particular time, is unreasonable. It is unnecessary to prove from these incidents that healing *is* available in response to faith; it is enough to show that they fail to prove healing is *not* available.

When the cases of Paul's thorn, Trophimus and Timothy are no longer argued in this way, there is nothing in the New Testament that qualifies the rule and practice of healing. And if it is still seriously maintained that they are exceptions, then equally seriously it can be maintained that the general rule is the otherwise unanimous testimony of the New Testament.

The will of God

It is frequently said that we do not know the will of God; therefore we cannot pray with undoubting faith that God will answer in the affirmative, so we have to conclude our prayer with the proviso "if it be thy will."

That we have to pray according to God's will if our prayers are to be answered is not in question. Nor is the fact that there are times when we do not know God's will. But there are many matters on which we *can* know God's will, because it is revealed in the Bible. His will for us is contained in "his precious and very great promises",[22] and we search the scriptures to see what these promises are. Once we determine what they are, we can appropriate them by the prayer of faith.

Often the phrase, "not my will, but thine, be done"[23] is used to create a false dichotomy. It is agreed that we must pray according to God's will. But his will is revealed to us in his promises; his promises reveal his will. So as we accept his promises by faith, we are praying according to his will.

Two writers said recently, "There are magnificent promises in the scripture to do with prayer. Take James 5:15, where we read, '…the prayer of faith will save the sick man, and the Lord will raise him up…' These are encouragements to faith in God, for this is a necessity in prayer." Yet they then continued, "But of course we must realise that God does not give us the things which are contrary to his will."[24]

The view that "there are magnificent promises in the scripture to do with prayer," but that it may not be God's will for us to have them in reality, is a contradiction in terms. It runs contrary to the basic concept of a promise-making and promise-keeping God. Our whole relationship with God is built on the "magnificent promises in the scripture." Without them we have no assurance of God's blessing — for salvation or anything else. We are "partakers of the promise in Christ Jesus through the gospel".[25] "All the promises of God find their Yes in him... Amen."[26] If God's will and provision are conveyed to us in one promise, then they are conveyed in every promise. If we are to appropriate one promise by faith, then we are to appropriate every promise by faith. We are not referring, of course, to promises that expressly belong to the future.[27]

In James 5: 14,15, as we have already seen, *there is a most clear promise of healing.* And this is part of a *wholly consistent revelation of this matter in the New Testament.*

*   *   *

It is clear that none of these four common objections can be sustained. A critical examination shows them to be weak and misleading. They have been brought out so often and for so long that we assume them to be valid. We adopt them readily because they seem at first sight to be reasonable, and perhaps without realising it, because they excuse us from becoming involved in something which would make very great demands on us, and which we are not prepared to face.

11

Only Believe

The prayer of faith

OUR THESIS HAS developed to the point where we are able to affirm that healing is a present provision of God, and that we are able to appropriate it by faith. We now turn our attention to the way in which we are to exercise faith in prayer. The chapters on faith in the pastoral section of the book need to be taken into account at this point.

James 5:15 states that it is "the prayer of faith" that enables the Lord to "raise up" the sick person. Our Lord illustrated what it means to have faith in prayer by his cursing of the fig tree. "Have faith in God. Truly I say to you, whoever says to this mountain, 'Be taken up and cast into the sea,' and does not doubt in his heart, but believes that what he says will come to pass, it will be done for him. Therefore I tell you, whatever you ask in prayer, believe that you have received it, and it will be yours."[1]

For prayer to be answered, God requires that *we believe we receive these things, so that we do not doubt in our heart.* To conclude a prayer with the proviso "if it be thy will" expresses doubt straight away. Whatever reasons are advanced for concluding a prayer this way, they are wrongly applied if they negate faith as God requires it to be exercised. Healing in the New Testament was always prayed for with complete assurance that it was going to eventuate, however serious the sickness or incapacity. It was never associated in thought or word with the proviso "if it be thy will." Our Lord's utterance "not my will, but thine, be done" is, with respect, irrelevant, because it concerns suffering, not sickness. In any case, as far as healing is concerned, there is an express promise which reveals God's will on this matter.

Those who claim that doctrine is deduced only from the epistles and not from narrative, are flatly contradicted by the epistle statement "all scripture is...profitable for teaching".[2] This cannot mean less than that narrative is doctrine-in-practice. And in regard to healing as practised in the New Testament, narrative explains the doctrine of how to pray for healing in a conclusive way.

The time comes for us all, of course, when it is God's will that we depart this life. We have a sickness that leads to death. Because of this, it could be said that we can never be sure whether or not the sickness we are experiencing at any one time is our last sickness. How then can we believe for healing so that we do not doubt? Do we not have to show our faith by saying "if it be thy will"?

What does the Bible have to say on this question? The same question was just as real for the church in New Testament times, but it did not affect the assurance with which the early Christians prayed for healing. The negative did not compromise the positive; they did not make a synthesis between them. Rather, the prayer of faith as it is defined in the scripture narratives was always the operative dimension. If some still feel that the question remains unanswered, then their problem is with what the Bible says.

Even so, no one has that difficulty when it comes to

drawing on the medical resource. Without hesitation we will draw upon all that medicine provides for healing in every sickness that we have — including that which leads to our death. In so doing, we take it for granted that we are acting according to God's will. Why, then, do we feel that we should pray differently? The practice of medicine and the practice of faith for healing have exactly the same intention and stem from the same understanding of God's will. They both affirm that God has given us life, and that we have a right and a duty to preserve it for as long as God permits it to remain.

If, on the other hand, it is reverently believed that the sick person has come to the end of his life span (and presumably this is reflected in the medical treatment), one no longer prays for healing. Rather does prayer accept the blessing of God appropriate to the circumstances. In this connection, we need more awareness that, to the Christian, death is not an enemy to be put off at all costs. It is God's last and greatest gift — that of going to be with him in the grace of Christ and the comfort of the Holy Spirit.

The point also needs to be made that when one prays in faith, it is remarkable how much discernment is given by the Spirit as to how to pray and minister appropriately. Supposed difficulties in theory do not usually prove to be difficulties in practice in this ministry. When one acts in faith, God guides and over-rules.

Whose responsibility is it to exercise faith?

Christ said that if the sick person had faith, this would enable him to be healed. "According to your faith be it done to you."[3] "Take heart, daughter; your faith has made you well."[4] Paul at Lystra, looking at the man who had been a cripple from birth, and "seeing that he had faith to be made well, said in a loud voice, 'Stand upright on your feet!'"[5]

We see nothing wrong in encouraging a person who is in bondage to sin to have faith for salvation and freedom. Indeed, we do not know any other approach. In the same way, there is nothing wrong in encouraging a sick person to have faith for healing.

There is also much in the New Testament about vicarious faith for the sick. "Is any among you sick? Let him call for the elders of the church, and let them pray over him...."[6] In the story recorded in Mark 2:1-12, where the four men brought their friend to Christ for healing, we are told, "When Jesus saw *their* faith, he said, 'My son, your sins are forgiven...rise, take up your pallet and walk!'" It was the faith of the four men that was used, as much for sin — "your sins are forgiven" — as for sickness — "take up your pallet and walk."

There is another important illustration in Matthew 17:14-21. The disciples had failed to heal a boy, but when the boy's father brought him to Christ, he was healed straight away. In the subsequent discussion, the Lord said it was the disciples' unbelief that prevented the healing. He did not blame the child or the parent, but those who had prayed the prayer of faith.

But though it was the apostles who were rebuked for their "little faith", it should be noted that Jesus also looked to the father to have faith. "All things are possible to him who believes."[7] This point is also brought out in the James passage. While it is the elders who are responsible for praying the prayer of faith, the sick person has to have faith enough to call them. The relevance of belief and unbelief in those being ministered to is graphically brought out by our Lord's ministry in his home town of Nazareth. The unbelieving inhabitants rendered almost ineffective even the perfect faith of Christ. Ultimately, it was a question of the faith of those ministered to, and not of him who ministered to them.

On the pastoral level, it is recognised that pain and anxiety often prevent the sick person from having faith, and it only compounds the problem to ask him to do what he is incapable of doing. But at least he must have enough faith to want others to have faith for him. When this is done, the responsibility for subsequent faith lies with "the elders of the church", or the individuals performing this role.

Whose responsibility is it then to exercise faith? There is no general rule. Faith is to be exercised by those who can have faith. In these illustrations, it is exercised by the sick person, by those acting on his behalf, or by those ministering to him. Vicarious faith is effective when it complements the faith of the sick person. Conversely, unbelief in those being ministered to can render impotent even perfect faith in those who pray from the "outside".

Progressive faith

Though divine healing may be immediate, its progressive character should be clearly understood. We need to keep in mind two things said by our Lord: firstly, that healing is part of the kingdom of God; and secondly, that the essential nature of the kingdom is to grow. This means that healing can come like the growing of a plant; minutely small at first, but in the long run full-grown. These points were adequately made in earlier chapters, and there is no need to go into that detail again.

Our Lord's healing of the blind man at Beth-saida[8] has this progressive character. After he had been prayed for the first time, the man said that he could see men but not clearly. They looked like tree trunks walking around. Then Christ laid on hands the second time, and the man saw everything perfectly.

If you may need to pray twice there is no reason why you may not pray any number of times, and once there is an interval it does not matter whether it is long or short. And if this can apply when the perfect faith of Christ was employed, how much more will it apply when our very imperfect faith is being relied on for prayer to be answered.

The point needs to be made that it is our *faith* that is progressive. In principle, the provision of God is there as soon as we believe and in proportion to our belief. This was made clear in the ministry of our Lord. It was at the time they believed[9] and it was according to or in proportion to their belief[10] that the healing was made effective. It is unscriptural to say that someone is healed "in God's time" if what is meant is different from this. It is our faith that needs to grow; the healing grows in proportion to faith and in consequence. In speaking about progressive healing, or the progressive answer to any promise of God, we should more correctly refer to it as progressive faith.

Much of the healing experienced today is drawn on in this progressive way. This, incidentally, is often the factor which makes it difficult to testify to healing in a convincing way. But where time is on our side, and the progressive aspect is understood, there is no limit to what can be accomplished, even though the mountain is big and faith is small. We have already seen in Part I a number of testimonies of healing which show how this works in practice, and many more could be given.

The progressive answer to prayer is understood and accepted in areas other than healing. And it is none the less seen to be an answer because it is progressive. A good illustration is in conversion. Some are converted in a moment — the change is immediate, complete and lasting. This is the kind usually described in the New Testament. But many who are converted today find it a more gradual process — again, "first the blade, then the ear..."[11] Yet we do not regard it as different in principle from conversion as described in the New Testament. Factors readily spring to mind to explain what difference there is, and these are universally understood and accepted.

It is only reasonable to expect the same understanding and acceptance when it comes to the progressive answer to prayer for healing.

12

Where There is no Vision...

WE WILL NOW examine as fairly as possible the alternative explanation put forward by those who hold that divine healing is not for today.

This alternative viewpoint begins with the premise that Christ healed to validate his Messiahship and his power to forgive sins. This reason was obviously personal to him alone, so it follows that healing does not relate to us in the same way. No further validation of Christ's authority is necessary, and in any case we could add nothing to what he has already done. No one has healed people as Christ healed them.

This view goes on to claim that the reason why the apostles and others healed was to validate the church, but once this was done, there was no further need for this sign, and so it was withdrawn. It is maintained that because the references to healing are predominantly in the gospels and Acts, and that there are only two references to healing in the rest of the New Testament, this could imply that healing was already in decline when these later events were recorded. The fact that healing has not been in common evidence since the third century is said to further confirm the probability that it is not intended for the on-going church. In any case, such healing as does occur today cannot be sufficiently identified with the type of healing recorded in the New Testament to justify the title "divine healing".

Those who expound this position, also point out that our Lord's statement that the kingdom of God is among us needs to be balanced by the fact that sin is still a present reality. Perfection of blessing is denied us in this life because we do not have complete and continuous victory over "the world rulers of this present darkness".[1] The assurance of God's perfect blessing is something that we can only anticipate in the life to come.

It is further affirmed that to conclude a prayer for healing with the words "if it be thy will" is not a prayer of doubt, but one of victorious faith: a faith prepared to leave the ultimate issues with God; a faith ready for death; a faith not stimulated by favourable results, but by complete acceptance of the final outcome — whether in sickness or health, life or death.

These assertions must be looked at critically. For too long they have been accepted without question. That Christ healed to validate his Messiahship is true, but it is not the only reason why he healed; it was *one* reason. The whole truth is that there were many reasons why he healed, and this was one of them. (This was discussed in Chapter 1 of this theological section.) Despite the reasons that were exclusive to Christ, the fact is that he committed the same healing ministry to his followers. This personal factor of validating his Messiahship was therefore not the definitive reason for his healings as some claim it to be.

There is nothing in the New Testament to lend substance to the idea that the disciples healed to validate the Christian church. This is a classic illustration of what is meant by a "tradition of man". When argument is built on that kind of reason, it is as useless as it is misleading. Theological exposition must always be concerned with what is contained in the scriptures.

Neither is there one word in the New Testament to say or suggest that healing was to be withdrawn. On the contrary, Paul's statement that there are gifts of healing, and James' statement that there is a healing ministry in the church, make it clear and definite that healing was intended to continue. As with Christ's ministry of healing, the only requirement was "the prayer of faith".[2]

On the matter of declining references to healing as the New Testament progresses, the same thing can be said about baptism and the Lord's supper. If it be a guide, the words "baptism" and "to baptise" are used approximately eighty times in the gospels and Acts, and less than twenty in the rest of the New Testament. The Lord's supper is referred to a dozen times in the gospels and Acts, and once in the epistles. Yet no one deduces from this that the use of the sacraments was already declining as the New Testament period progressed. It is then inconsistent to make that deduction as it concerns healing.

It is agreed that the supernatural gifts of the Spirit, including healing, are not in common evidence today. But what is the real explanation? Dr Evelyn Frost, in her book *Christian Healing*,[3] says that if we attempt to assess the work of Jesus Christ in history, not merely in regard to the value of each manifestation, but from an overall point of view, we see that:

> The temperature of the spiritual life of the church was the index of her power to heal. As far as the ante-Nicene church is concerned, the history of her spiritual life is one of decline from the high peaks of the apostolic days to the lower spiritual level at which controversy, apostasy and heresy were formidable weakening factors in her life. Side by side with this growing weakness can be seen a decline in the power of healing.

Once these other factors accounting for the decline in healing are introduced, the whole question is thrown open in a new way. The gifts of the Spirit, including healing, are "the manifestation of the Spirit".[4] And we have the greatest need,

as Bishop John Howe, Secretary-General of the Anglican
Consultative Council, has said, "to know what are the factors
that will enable the Holy Spirit to be stirred up or released in
our contemporary situation."[5] This will involve an historical
study, like that of Frost, as well as a scriptural one.

Might it not be that we need a fresh vision of what is
available, remembering that God is the same yesterday, today
and forever? We also need the repentance, faith and obedience to increasingly appropriate these provisions. This may
well require a re-drawing of our personal and pastoral lives. It
is simply not enough for a tiny minority in the church to
believe. This is the point made by Frost. It is the whole body
of Christ which has to be involved. My own conviction is that
the main single reason for the lack of these ministries in the
church today, in all their New Testament reality, is that the
body of Christ as a whole does not really believe in them.

On the question of identifying what happens now with
what happened then, we can only answer that if we were
required to measure what happens in our contemporary
church life against the experience of the church in the early
days of Holy Spirit power, then there would be very little in
any area that we could find the same! For example, very few
are converted in our western church today — nothing like
what we see described in the early church. But no one
suggests that what happens today is invalid because of that.
Instead we rejoice for what blessing there is, re-examine our
position and move in for action. If we are going to be
consistent, then what is good for conversion should be good
for healing.

The question raised by the present reality of sin, and the
qualification this makes to the kingdom of God, is more
apparent than real. Sin was just as real in the primitive
church when healing was available in response to faith. When
it came to the prayer of faith for healing, the reality of sin did
not qualify the kingdom of God. As with the problem of
physical death (see Chapter 11, *The prayer of faith*,) the

negative did not affect the positive. Again, the disciples did not make a synthesis between them; again, the kingdom of God and the commission of Christ were the operative dimensions. The disciples prayed, and always prayed, in full assurance that healing would eventuate because of their faith.

We must of course, respect those who believe that it is an affirmation of faith to conclude their prayer for healing with the words "if it be thy will", because they do so with meaningful sincerity. We can all think of devout Christians who have faced sickness, and who have faced death, with that affirmation in their heart and on their lips. But the difficulty with this view, and the reason why it cannot be accepted, is the fact that it was not the way faith was exercised for healing in the New Testament. As we have just noted, the early Christians prayed, and prayed always, with complete conviction that healing would eventuate because of their faith.

If those who speak against the healing ministry still argue that they do not believe in these ministries because they do not see them, one can only reply that they do not see them because they do not believe in them. Faith always precedes sight; and it is faith in the statement of the scriptures that "the gifts...of God are irrevocable."[6]

13

Conclusions

IN A SHORT study such as this, it may not be right to talk about "conclusions". But an attempt has been made to look objectively at the picture which the New Testament presents, and to take that as our rule and guide. If any aspect of New Testament revelation has been neglected or misunderstood, the correction would be welcomed.

We have seen that there were many reasons why Christ healed. Some were personal to him, others, such as the expression and demonstration of the kingdom, are common to all Christians at all times. It is clear that he did not regard the healing ministry as unique to himself, because the same ministry is expressly committed to the twelve and the seventy.

Neither is there any reason to suggest that the ministry was unique to the twelve and to the seventy. On the contrary, the ministries of Philip and Stephen show that it was normal for any Christian to both preach and heal, and for that ministry to be essentially the same as that of the apostles in its effect. Paul specifically stated that there are gifts of healing for members of the body of Christ. The church-oriented statement of James goes on to show that this ministry was intended to be exercised by the local church.

With regard to the objections that are raised, it is clear that there is value in suffering, but the New Testament description of suffering does not include sickness. Whatever value there is in sickness was never urged upon the innumerable people ministered to in the scripture narrative. In no case did it limit the availability of their healing in response to faith. When we pray for healing we are praying according to the will of God.

The objection to the dependability of healing that is drawn from Paul's thorn is discredited at every point of examination. It has to be rejected, the more so because it would compromise what Christ taught and committed to the church. The same applies to Trophimus and Timothy.

The prayer of faith is to be acted on as it is in the doctrine-in-action narratives. We are to believe that we have received these things so that we do not doubt in our heart. Our Lord said, "Only believe."[1] Where the disciples failed to heal, Christ said it was because of their "little faith".[2]

Faith can be exercised by the sick person or by those acting on his behalf. It may be shown simply by asking others to have faith for him. It is then the responsibility of "the elders" to pray the prayer of faith.

When the progressive aspect of healing is understood and lived out, it does much to provide experiential testimony of healing today. The "growth" principle is understood and accepted without question in every other area of answered prayer; it is only being sensible and consistent to apply it to healing.

The argument that healing and the other spiritual gifts are not intended for the church today, because they are not always seen as described in the New Testament, is rejected because it is a denial of the statement that God's gifts have been given in permanence. If they are not seen then the failure is on our part. We have advanced Dr Frost's thesis that it is an historical fact that when the church lost "the unity of the Spirit in the bond of peace"[3] it lost much of the power of God.

In our judgment the other points that are made against the healing ministry today do not stand up to a reasoned examination. By contrast we believe that the case for divine healing is a straight-forward exposition of the word of God.

Taken as a whole, this study of the healing ministry in the New Testament affirms that healing is as available today as it was in the early days of Christianity. The wholly consistent testimony of scripture, the unqualified promise in James that the prayer of faith will raise up the sick man, and the present reality of the kingdom, are our reasons for believing that healing is a continuing resource in the church and is available in response to faith.

It does not even have to be asked for. Why ask for what you already have? It only needs to be understood and accepted. The kingdom of God *is* in the midst of you. Your healing *is* within you.

Appendix to Part II

The Translation and Use of Astheneō

In James 5:14, the Greek word *astheneō* is translated as "sick". "The prayer of faith will save the sick man..." In 2 Corinthians 12: 9,10, the same word *astheneō* is translated "weaknesses". St Paul said, "I will all the more gladly boast of my weaknesses..."

Critics of the healing ministry maintain that it is inconsistent to translate *astheneō* in James as "sick", so affirming a promise of healing, while refusing to translate Paul's "weaknesses" as "sickness", which could suggest that it may not be God's will to heal. Certainly it would be arbitrary indeed to translate the word as "sickness" in one passage and "non-sickness" in another, unless there were reasons for doing so.

But there *are* good reasons for translating *astheneō* in different ways. The Greek word has many meanings, and the context has to be used to ascertain the particular meaning being employed at any one time. *Context is always the final arbiter as to the meaning intended in the use of a word.* Some of the meanings of *astheneō* are: sickness; physical weakness (as contrasted with physical strength); character weakness; weakness in faith; human frailty; weakness of understanding; weakness of the law; weakness through adversity. A complete list of the meanings used in the New Testament is attached.

The context of *astheneō* in 2 Corinthians chapters 11-12 has no connection with "sickness". Paul was speaking of "insults, hardships, persecutions, calamities" and the like. We have already seen from our study that this is the suffering or persecution that comes from being a Christian. It is for this reason that the various versions of the Bible always translate *astheneō* in this passage as "infirmities" or "weaknesses", and never as "sickness".

Our examination of what was meant by the "thorn", which was the cause of Paul's weaknesses, showed that there is no reason to maintain that it was sickness, and every reason to maintain that it was non-sickness or suffering. This means that in both its immediate and wider contexts, *astheneō* in this passage is required to be translated as "weakness through adversity" or non-sickness.

On the other hand, the context of James 5: 14,15 is plainly about sickness. Anointing with oil was a sacramental act directly associated with healing. (See Mark 6: 12,13.) The point is sometimes made that this passage lends credence to medical practice, the use of oil being an early form of medical treatment — as in the case of the man who fell among thieves. Whether this is so or not, the passage is accepted as referring to sickness. "The prayer of faith" was also intimately and obviously associated with sickness and healing, and equally clearly not associated with the other meanings of *astheneō*. It was certainly not associated with "weakness through adversity" or "suffering" in the New Testament sense of that word.

Altogether, the contexts clearly show that *astheneō* in James 5: 14,15 means "sickness", and that in 2 Corinthians 12: 7-10 it is "weakness through adversity" or "suffering".

*   *   *

The following are the varying uses of Astheneō *in the New Testament.*

A. *In the sense of ordinary illness:*
Matthew 8:17 10:18 25:39,43,44.
Mark 6:56
Luke 4:40 5:15 8:2 9:2 10:9 13:11,12
John 4:46 5:5 11:1-4,6
Acts 5:15 9:37 19:12 28:9

1 Corinthians 11:30	That is why many of you are *weak* and ill.
Galatians 4:13	It was because of a bodily *ailment* that I preached the gospel to you at first.
Philippians 2:26,27	Epaphroditus...you heard that he was *ill...ill* near to death.
1 Timothy 5:23	Use a little wine for your stomach and your frequent *ailments*.
2 Timothy 4:20	Trophimus I left *ill* at Miletus.
James 5:14	Is any among you *sick*?

B. *In the sense of physical weakness:*

1 Corinthians 15:43	The body is sown in *weakness*, it is raised in power.
1 Peter 3:7	bestowing honour on the woman as the *weaker* sex.

C. *In the sense of character weakness, or faith weakness, human frailty, or weakness of understanding etc.:*

Matthew 26:41 / Mark 14:38	The spirit indeed is willing, but the flesh is *weak*.
Acts 20:35	By so toiling one must help the *weak*.
Romans 4:19	Abraham...did not *weaken* in faith.
Romans 6:19	I am speaking in human terms, because of your natural *limitations*.
Romans 8:26	The Spirit helps us in our *weakness*; for we do not know how to pray as we ought.

Romans 14:1,2,21	As for the man who is *weak* in faith.
Romans 15:1	We who are strong ought to bear with the *failings* of the weak.
1 Corinthians 1:25	The *weakness* of God is stronger than men. (i.e. the death on the cross.)
1 Corinthians 1:27	God chose what is *weak* in the world to shame the strong.
1 Corinthians 2:3	I was with you in *weakness* and in much fear and trembling.
1 Corinthians 8:7, 9-12	Their conscience, being *weak*, is defiled.
1 Corinthians 9:22	To the *weak* I became *weak*, that I might win the *weak*.
2 Corinthians 10:10	His letters are weighty and strong but his bodily presence is *weak* and his speech of no account.
1 Thessalonians 5:14	Encourage the faint hearted, help the *weak*.
Hebrews 4:15	We have not a high priest who is unable to sympathise with our *weaknesses*.
Hebrews 5:2	Every high priest...can deal gently with the ignorant and wayward, since he himself is beset with *weakness*.
Hebrews 7:28	The law appoints men in their *weakness* as high priests.
Hebrews 11:34	Who through faith...won strength out of *weakness*.

D. *In the sense of weakness of the law and of elemental spirits:*

Romans 8:3	God has done what the law, *weakened* by the flesh could not do.
Galatians 4:9	Now that you have come to know God... how can you turn back again to the *weak* and beggarly elemental spirits.
Hebrews 7:18	A former commandment is set aside because of its *weakness* and uselessness.

E. *The references in 2 Corinthians 11:21 to 12:10:*

11:21	We were too *weak* for that...labours, imprisonments, beatings, death, lashes, stoned, ship-wrecked, journeys, danger, toil, hardship, hunger, thirst, cold, exposure.
11:29	My anxiety for all the churches. Who is *weak* and I am not *weak*?
11:30	If I must boast, I will boast of the things that show my *weakness*...(vs. 33) I was let down in a basket through a window in the wall.
12:5	On my own behalf I will not boast, except of my *weaknesses*.
12:7-9	A thorn was given me in the flesh, a messenger of Satan, to harass me, to keep me from being too elated. Three times I besought the Lord about this... but he said to me, "My grace is sufficient for you, for my power is made perfect in *weakness*." I will all the more gladly boast of my *weaknesses* that the power of Christ may rest upon me. For the sake of Christ, then, I am content with *weaknesses*, insults, hardships, persecutions, and calamities; for when I am *weak*, then I am strong.

References

PART I

Chapter 1

1. Mark 4:28
2. Mark 9:23
3. John 14:27
4. Hebrews 13:5
5. 2 Corinthians 5:17
6. James 1:4
7. Matthew 6:10
8. 2 Peter 1:4
9. John 5:39
10. 1 John 1:9
11. Luke 4: 38-40
12. Matthew 20: 33,34
13. John 9:4
14. John 14:12
15. Acts 3: 1-10
16. Mark 11: 20-26
17. James 5:15
18. Mark 4:28

Chapter 2

1. John 20:29
2. Ephesians 2:1
3. Acts 16: 30,31
4. 2 Corinthians 5:7
5. Mark 9:23
6. Matthew 9:29

Chapter 3

1. Mark 11:25
2. Mark 11:24
3. Mark 11:25
4. Job 3:25
5. 2 Timothy 1:7 (A.V.)
6. 1 John 4:18
7. Genesis 32:26
8. James 1:7
9. Mark 4:28
10. Luke 10:9
11. Matthew 9:29
12. James 1:4

Chapter 4

1. John 20:23

Chapter 5

1. Ephesians 5:18
2. John 3:6
3. John 3:7
4. Ephesians 3:16
5. Acts 9:17
6. Acts 22: 8,10
7. Acts 9:15
8. Acts 9:7
9. Acts 19:2
10. Acts 8:16
11. Acts 8:17
12. 2 Timothy 3:16
13. Philippians 3:13
14. 1 Peter 5:8
15. Acts 4:30
16. Mark 5:36

Chapter 6

1. 1 Corinthians 12: 14-26
2. 1 Corinthians 12:11
3. James 5:14
4. 1 Timothy 2:4
5. Book of Common Prayer.
6. Colossians 4:2
7. Matthew 17: 14-21/Mark 9:29
8. Mark 9:23
9. Genesis 32:26
10. Job 1:21
11. Philippians 3:13
12. Acts 4: 29,30

PART II

Chapter 7

1. Luke 6: 17-19
2. Matthew 4:23
3. Mark 6:56
4. Acts 10:38
5. John 9:4
6. Mark 1: 40,41
7. John 4:34
8. Mark 1:41
9. Matthew 14:14
10. Matthew 8: 16,17
11. Mark 2: 1-12
12. Matthew 11: 3-5
13. John 11:4
14. John 9:3
15. John 9: 35-38
16. John 14:11
17. Matthew 9: 27-30
18. Mark 5: 25-34
19. Matthew 8: 5-13
20. Matthew 9: 18-26
21. Matthew 13:57
22. Matthew 13:58
23. Mark 6: 4,5
24. 1 John 3:8
25. Luke 8: 26-36
26. Matthew 12:22
27. Luke 13:16
28. Revelation 11:15
29. Revelation 21:4
30. Luke 17: 20,21
31. Luke 13: 18-21
32. Mark 4:28
33. Matthew 12:28
34. Luke 10:9
35. Luke 12:31
36. Luke 12:32
37. 1 Peter 2:24
38. Luke 10:9

Chapter 8

1.	Matthew 10: 7,8	18.	Acts 9: 36-42
	Mark 6:7	19.	Acts 14: 8-10
	Mark 16: 17,18	20.	Acts 16: 16-18
	Luke 9: 1,2	21.	Acts 20: 7-12
	Luke 10: 8,9	22.	Acts 28: 3-6
2.	Matthew 10:1	23.	Acts 28:8
3.	Luke 9:2	24.	Acts 6:8
4.	Mark 6: 12,13	25.	Acts 8: 5-8
5.	Luke 9:6	26.	Acts 14:3
6.	Luke 10: 8,9	27.	Acts 19: 11-12
7.	Luke 10: 17-20	28.	Acts 28:9
8.	Matthew 10: 1-16	29.	Acts 9:34
9.	Mark 6:7	30.	Acts 14: 8-10
10.	Luke 10: 1-12	31.	Acts 3: 1-16
11.	Luke 9: 1-6	32.	Acts 14: 8-18
12.	Mark 16: 9-20	33.	Acts 6:8
13.	Luke 10:19	34.	Acts 8: 6,7
14.	Acts chs. 2,5,10,16,19,28	35.	Acts 14:3
15.	Acts 3: 1-16	36.	Acts 9: 17,18
16.	Acts 9: 10-19	37.	Luke 10:19
17.	Acts 9: 32-35		

Chapter 9

1.	Mark 16: 17,18	2.	Hebrews 11:6

Chapter 10

1.	Hebrews 5:8	13.	2 Corinthians 12:7
2.	Hebrews 5:9	14.	2 Corinthians 12:10
3.	Acts 5:41	15.	2 Corinthians 12:7
4.	1 Peter 3: 14,17	16.	2 Corinthians 12:9
5.	1 Thessalonians 2: 14	17.	2 Timothy 4:20
6.	Acts 9: 15,16	18.	1 Timothy 5:23
7.	John 13:16	19.	Philippians 2: 25-30
8.	James 5: 13,14	20.	1 Timothy 2:4
9.	2 Corinthians 12: 1-10	21.	Matthew 17:20
10.	Acts 14: 9	22.	2 Peter 1:4
11.	Numbers 33:55	23.	Luke 22:42
12.	Joshua 23:13.	24.	*Quest for Power*
	see also 2 Samuel 23:6		Barnett and Jensen p. 90
			ANZEA Publishers, Australia.

25. Ephesians 3:6   27. e.g. John 6:54
26. 2 Corinthians 1:20

Chapter 11

1. Mark 11:22-24   7. Mark 9:23
2. 2 Timothy 3:16   8. Mark 8:22-25
3. Matthew 9:29   9. Matthew 9:13
4. Matthew 9:22   10. Matthew 9: 27-30
5. Acts 14: 9.10   11. Mark 4:28
6. James 5:14

Chapter 12

1. Ephesians 6:12   4. 1 Corinthians 12:7
2. James 5:15   5. Synod Sermon in Sydney
3. *Christian Healing* Frost p.50   Cathedral, May 1973
   Hodder and Stoughton   6. Romans 11:29

Chapter 13

1. Mark 5:36   3. Ephesians 4:3
2. Matthew 17:20